# THE SHITTY TRUTH ABOUT MANAGEMENT

# The Shitty Truth About

# Management

**NIKKI KATZ**

Katz Chaos
Publishing

# Disclaimer

This book is a work of non-fiction based on real events. However, names, identifying details, and certain scenarios have been changed or fictionalized to protect the privacy of individuals. Any resemblance to actual persons, living or dead, is purely coincidental.

The opinions expressed within these pages are solely those of the author and do not reflect the views of any past or present employer.

This book is intended for entertainment and informational purposes only.

This book is dedicated to all the hard workers who've been smothered by inefficiencies, beaten down by corporate nonsense, and thrown headfirst into absolute chaos.

I see you.

I've felt your frustrations.

Your feelings are valid.

This one's for you.

# CONTENTS

*Disclaimer*                                             iv

*Dedication*                                              v

**Welcome to the Chaos**                                 1

1  **A Shitty Start**                                     5

2  **A Pain in the Ass**                                 13

3  **The Ghosts of Severance Packages Past**            23

4  **The Corporate Circus of Bullshit**                 39

5  **The Complaint Chronicles**                         59

6  **Welcome to the Boys' Club**                        73

7  **Navigating Your Boss's Inefficiencies**            84

8  **The Toxic Workplace Survival Guide**               98

9  **Neurodiversity in the Workplace**                 108

| 10 | **Times I've Fucked Up** | **117** |
| 11 | **When The Office isn't just a Sitcom** | **125** |
| | **So, You Still Want to Be a Manager?** | **135** |

*About the Author*      138

# WELCOME TO THE CHAOS

**W**elcome to management.
Nope, that's not right.

**Welcome to the chaos.**

Congrats! You've made it into a management position. Maybe you fought for this promotion. Maybe it was forced upon you. Either way, if you're picking up this book, you're probably looking for some kind of guidance on how to be an effective leader.

Well, let me be the first to break the news:
Managing teams, leading people, and being a figurehead for your company is not what you think it's going to be.

This is not a corporate leadership book. I have no airy-fairy motivational speeches to offer you. There will be no inspiring TED Talk quotes or "5 Simple Steps to Being a Great Leader" bullshit.

What you're about to read is a no-nonsense, brutally honest, occasionally disgusting, and often hilarious deep dive into what management *actually* is. And maybe—just maybe—if you squint really hard and reframe the situation entirely, you'll find there *are* some beautiful things that come out of the managerial chaos.

*(Emphasis on the squinting.)*

## Before You Dive In, Some Important Context

I'm not holding back. Everything you're about to read actually happened.

The names? Changed. The ridiculousness? All real, unfortunately.

This book includes:
**Swear words.** Lots of them.
**Stories of fecal matter.** More than you'd expect. Possibly more than you'd like.
**HR nightmares.** The kind that keep corporate lawyers up at night.
**Buttholes.** Because, for some reason, management involves an unreasonable amount of buttholes.

*This is your official trigger and sensitivity warning.*

Since 2013, I've been managing and running fitness facilities and rock climbing gyms. That might not seem important now, but it will when you're wondering why on earth I keep ending up in situations involving bodily fluids and completely unnecessary workplace disasters.

And while I'd love to tell myself that this level of managerial chaos is exclusive to the fitness industry, I know better. You corporate keyboard executives are dealing with your own versions of this shit, just (hopefully) in a much less literal sense.

## What I Thought Management Would Be vs. What It Actually Is

When I first clawed my way into management, I thought I'd be:

- **Making meaningful decisions**
- **Engaging with my team and clients**
- **Shaping the direction of the company**

*And technically, yes.* I do those things…about 5% of the time.

The other 95%?

- **Wading knee-deep in sewage** (*sometimes literally*).
- **Navigating last-minute call-offs due to planetary alignment.**
- **Listening to employees share deeply personal medical emergencies that I absolutely did not ask to know about.**
- **Refereeing Nerf battles with my boss.**
- **Approving time off for butt surgery.**
- **Teaching a professionally misogynistic electrician how to operate a boom lift.**

Management is not what you think it is.

But somehow, amidst all the ridiculousness, real leadership lessons emerge.

You learn to be adaptable. You realize that while fun is important, professionalism matters too. You also learn which employees will overshare about their bowel movements the moment they feel comfortable around you.

Welcome to the chaos of management.

Strap in. Strap on. It's going to be a wild (and highly rewarding) ride.

# | 1 |

# A Shitty Start

## FROM BRIGHT-EYED OPTIMISM TO BAPTISM BY FECAL MATTER

My first "big break" in management happened in 2022. After several long years working as an assistant manager at a gym, a team of investors hired me to open, run, and manage their brand-new, multi-million dollar, state-of-the-art rock climbing facility. Super cool opportunity. Even cooler, I was brought in before the gym was finished being built. I helped manage the build and grand opening from the ground up. I got to hire my team, train them how I wanted, and conduct my first interviews in a half-constructed building while climbing walls were still being installed.

*(Core memory unlocked: building my team alongside the build of my facility.)*

Sounds too good to be true, right?

Definitely right.

Before my gym even opened to the public, it was decided that we would host the USA Climbing Youth National Championships. You don't need to know anything about climbing to know that this event is a big deal. Athletes and families travel from all over the country to compete. Thousands upon thousands of people would be coming through our facility every single day.

And the pressure was on. This was our first major event—our chance to prove ourselves. Everything needed to be perfect.

Here's the problem:

My beautiful, brand-new, multi-million dollar, state-of-the-art climbing gym had not been stress-tested yet.

Before Nationals, the building had barely accommodated 20 people at a time. Now, we were hosting thousands.

And let me tell you—the building did not pass the stress test.

# When Nationals Became a National Disaster

Bouldering finals had just started.

This was it. The main event. The gym was packed shoulder to shoulder, and the energy was through the roof. Everyone was watching the strongest youth climbers in the country fight for a national title.

I was stationed at the merch shop, boasting to anyone who would listen about my beautiful, brand-new, multi-million dollar, state-of-the-art climbing gym.

And then a coach sprinted up to me.

He was frazzled, panicked, and clearly debating whether or not to throw up. He blurted out something about the men's and women's bathrooms flooding.

I thanked him for the information and went to investigate.

A clogged toilet or two? Super manageable.

I was so, so wrong.

I stepped into the hallway leading to the bathrooms and—

Squish.

I looked down.

The entire hallway was sitting in two inches of water.

And as I got closer, the water only got deeper.

Then, the smell hit me.

It wasn't water.

The bathrooms were flooding with raw sewage.

Okay. It couldn't get worse than that, right?

Wrong. Even more wrong.

I later learned that there were rocks and debris stuck in our pipes. All the toilet paper, human feces, and god-knows-what-else got trapped—until it couldn't be trapped anymore.

Then, the pipes failed spectacularly.

And where did several inches of stagnant sewage water drain?

The basement.

Yes. The basement of my beautiful, brand-new, multi-million dollar, state-of-the-art climbing gym was now a literal pool of human waste.

*Mini Lesson: Always assume your worst-case scenario is possible, and plan for it. The universe has a sense of humor.*

## Crisis Management: Step 1 - Cry

Stop and ask yourself—what is the absolute **first** thing you would do as a manager in this situation?

- **Delegate cleanup?**
- **Call a professional sanitation crew?**
- **Announce an emergency closure?**

I did none of these things.

Instead, I stood in my shit-flooded basement, watched sewage cascade down the walls, and sobbed.

To be fair, what else do you do when your entire career milestone turns into an actual cesspool?

***Mini Lesson:*** *It's okay to cry in the face of absurdity. Just don't unpack and live there forever.*

## Crisis Management: Step 2 - Actually Fix It

But crying wasn't going to fix it.

And thank *every* god in existence for my absolutely incredible team because there was no way I could have handled this on my own.

I took a deep breath (through my mouth, obviously), wiped my tears, and went into full crisis management mode.

I divided up emergency tasks and delegated them across multiple employees and managers:

- **Communicate with visitors** - Apologize profusely, redirect people to nearby public restrooms (which we suddenly became very thankful for).
- **Rent port-a-potties** - Pay for rush delivery. Beg if necessary.
- **Call a professional cleaning crew** - Bribe them. Pay extra. Whatever it takes.
- **Call the plumbers** - Demand they come out that night. They did.
- **Post signs. So many signs.** Clearly mark all closed-off areas and alternative bathrooms.

*Mini Lesson: When there's no playbook, trust your instincts and lead with urgency.*
*No one trains you for a poop flood. There was no emergency binder with a section titled "What to Do When the Basement Becomes a Biohazard." I didn't have a manual—I just made the call, and we handled it.*

With the upstairs crisis under control, that left one final problem:

The basement.

## The Shittiest Task of All

There was no way I was going to ask a staff member to clean up actual human excrement in the basement.

...And there was no one above me to tag in for this particular shit show.

So I grabbed a mop, a bucket, and every last ounce of dignity I had left, and I went down into the sewage-filled depths of my beautiful, brand-new, multi-million dollar, state-of-the-art climbing gym.

And I cleaned it myself.

And I cried.

And then I dumped an unhealthy amount of bleach over every square inch of that basement.

*Mini Lesson: You don't get to skip the dirty work. Sometimes leadership is being the first one to grab the mop.*

## The Poop-Colored Silver Lining of Surviving My Shitty Start to Upper Management

**1.) When things break down, it's an opportunity to build better.** Yes, the plumbing got stronger after this disaster—but so did I. Through my own stressy, messy, poop-induced breakdown, I learned how to lead through absolute chaos. I became a stronger manager not because things went well, but because I survived when they didn't.

**2.) You cannot manage a crisis alone.** This would have been a full-blown PR disaster without my team. Their ability to pivot, troubleshoot, and rally in the face of literal shit is what kept our gym's reputation intact.

**3.) Leadership is a war zone. Choose your team wisely.** Nationals became a war story for our staff. The people who were in the trenches with me became fiercely loyal—not because I had all the answers, but because I didn't make them clean up poop.

Welcome to management. Strap in. It only gets worse from here.

# | 2 |

# A Pain in the Ass

## LITERALLY. IN MULTIPLE CASES.

**D**isclaimer:

The stories, along with the pain and medical conditions outlined in this chapter, are very real. My reactions and eye-twitch-inducing, forced responses of pure unfiltered professionalism are also very real. I would like to acknowledge that what these individuals went through was probably traumatizing for them (honestly, it was for me too), and rectal health is quite serious.

That being said, please seek the advice of a medical professional for your anal issues—**not your manager.**

## The First Incident: A Bleeding Disaster

There are certain things a manager expects to hear from their staff.

- *"Hey, I'm going to be late."*
- *"Hey, I need time off next week."*
- *"Hey, we're out of hand soap in the bathroom."*

What a manager does not expect to hear is:

*"Hey, my butthole is actively bleeding—what should I do?"*

And yet, in my years of managing gyms, I have somehow become the unwilling recipient of an alarming amount of butt-related confessions.

One day, an employee, we'll call him Pat, comes up to me and says:

"Nikki, I have a problem."

I was like, *"OK Pat, hit me with it."*
(Oh. He hit me with it. I regret challenging him with that statement.)

*"Well, I pooped in the family bathroom."*

I blinked. *"Um...congrats? In the toilet, I hope?"*

*"Well, it was really big."*

At this point, I'm thinking he just clogged the toilet. Annoying but manageable.

Then this man looks me dead in the eyes and says—

*"And now it's bleeding...a lot."*

A sick, foreboding feeling washed over me. *"Um...what's bleeding, Pat?"*
I already knew the answer. I didn't want the answer.

*"My asshole. And there's blood all over the family bathroom...and I don't know what to do."*

To which I respond (very calm and professionally, may I add):
*"Do you need medical attention? Do you need to sit down? CAN you even sit down?"*

I also had no idea what to do about the butt blood in the bathroom.

This particular story ends with Pat being OK (mostly), me giving him a full tutorial on where we keep the heavy-duty cleaning products, and him deep-cleaning the family bathroom.

I also like to think he sought medical attention after this *horribly* traumatic event.
(Though, honestly, I did not ask for a follow-up.)

To Pat's credit, that bathroom was spotless after he cleaned it.

*Mini Lesson: Staff will overshare—prepare accordingly. You're a manager, not a medical professional. Handle it with grace—but know when to draw the line.*

## The Abscess That Became a Saga

At the time, I thought Pat's bloody bathroom breakdown was a one-time thing. A fluke. A horrible, unfortunate anomaly.

But no.

It was merely the beginning.

*(Enter Andy, the man with a developing saga in his backside.)*

Unlike Pat, who came to me in a moment of crisis, Andy's situation unfolded over months.

It started small.

Then, much like his abscess, it grew.

Over several weeks, Andy made it clear to me that he had a pain in his ass.

Me, being the hopefully naive boss that I am, blissfully assumed this was a metaphor.

It was not a metaphor.

Andy stopped sitting at his desk. He could only stand. He began having a difficult time driving to work because it genuinely hurt him to sit down.

Then, he finally confided in me.

*"I have an abscess in my butt. I need surgery."*

So, Andy had surgery on his butt.

You'd think the story would end here, right?

Wrong.

This is a saga, after all.

When Andy returned from his medical procedure, we were back on track for a few weeks.
Until he once again was unable to sit without being in pain.

This time, however, he was in so much pain that his entire demeanor shifted.

Andy informed me that his once-anal-abscess had now turned into an anal fistula.

I, being the empathetic and idiotic boss that I am, asked:
*"What does that mean?"*

*(I should not have asked. I should never have asked.)*

In case you don't know what an anal fistula is, let me educate you (as Andy, unfortunately, educated me).

An anal fistula is an abnormal tunnel-like passage that connects the anal canal to the skin around the anus.

So, this may come as a surprise to you, but I am not a medical professional.
I had no prior knowledge of anal fistulas.

So when Andy—who, I cannot stress this enough, did NOT need to tell me, his boss, all these details—explained his diagnosis, my overworked and underpaid little squirrel brain came to one unavoidable conclusion:

He had developed a second butthole.

I know that's not technically what happened, but that's what my brain decided, and unfortunately, I had to live with that mental image.

To close out the saga of Andy's Anal Abscess, I had to approve time off for not one, but two medical rectal procedures.

And it became my direct responsibility to help cover Andy's administrative work while he got his second butthole removed.

*Mini Lesson:* *Medical emergencies should go to doctors, not your inbox. Support your staff—but redirect them to appropriate resources when personal health gets too personal.*

## The Man Who Took 45-Minute Poops

By this point, I had accepted that butthole-related conversations were just part of my job.

But somehow, against all odds, things got worse.

Enter Ben.

Employees had started noticing a pattern.

Whenever Ben was nowhere to be found, he was almost always in the bathroom.

So, out of sheer curiosity, I asked:
*"Ben, why do your bathroom breaks last for 45+ minutes?"*

Ben responded with the utmost sincerity:

*"Well, when I sit on the toilet and poop, after it comes out, I wait a bit to see if there's more. And there always is. So I just...wait to get it all out."*

Maybe I shouldn't have asked.

Maybe this was one of those managerial things I should have just let go.

But now I had to respond in a professional and HR-appropriate way, so I said:

*"Um, thank you for the information...but could you maybe not spend so much company time on the toilet?"*

And in the most sincere, honest response possible, he said:

*"Oh, I'm not trying to get out of work! I'm just trying to do my business...and sometimes it takes a while."*

And that was it. That was my breaking point. I had officially heard enough about butt holes and bowel movements.

*"Cool. Clock out when you poop."*

I didn't argue. I didn't fight it.

I had learned a valuable lesson:

I couldn't stop employees from talking about their butts. But I could, at the very least, stop them from getting paid for it.

*Mini Lesson:* *Set the tone, then set the policy. Sometimes the most effective HR solution is, "Clock out when you poop."*

# The Poop-Colored Silver Lining of Dealing With a Pain in Your Ass

**1.) Employees Will Overshare**—You Must Handle It With Grace (Or At Least a Straight Face).

No matter what industry you work in, employees will tell you things you absolutely did not ask to know. As a manager, it is not your job to be their doctor, therapist, or confession booth, but it *is* your job to navigate these conversations with as much professionalism as you can muster. Even when they involve blood, abscesses, or extremely detailed accounts of bodily functions—because, apparently, that's part of the gig.

**2.) Boundaries Are Crucial (Especially When It Comes to Butthole Disclosures).**

A workplace should be a safe, open environment—but not *this* open. Employees should feel comfortable communicating concerns, but some lines should never be crossed. The unspoken rule should be:

- If you feel compelled to share information about your butt, reconsider.
- If you insist on sharing, do NOT do it in front of clients.
- If you make another employee uncomfortable, it's time to stop talking.

Boundaries are key—and if an employee has a medical concern, they should be taking it to a doctor, not their manager.

## 3.) Management & HR Are a Tightrope Walk (And Sometimes You Fall Into the Abyss).

The fine line between managing people and absorbing their deeply personal problems is alarmingly thin. You are *technically* there to oversee operations, logistics, and team performance, yet somehow, you end up acting as a makeshift HR department, therapist, and sometimes, a rectal health consultant.

- Employees confide in you.
- You try to enforce boundaries.
- You fail.
- You end up approving butt surgery time off and implementing a new "clock out to poop" policy.
  Welcome to management.


This chapter should not exist.

No manager should have to navigate this level of oversharing, and yet, here we are.

# | 3 |

# The Ghosts of Severance Packages Past

## TALES FROM BEYOND THE TERMINA-TION LETTERS

Hiring people is supposed to make your life easier. In theory, the more people you hire, the more tasks you can delegate.

The problem? If you hire the wrong people, you will end up doing their job for them—and no one warns you about that part of management. And also their terrible attitude and work ethic has a lingering effect on your entire staff personnel…and their absolute bullshit may scar you as a manager just a bit…or at least cause you to question your sanity.

Let me introduce you to some of the severenced spirits that still haunt my managerial nightmares.

# The Dungeons & Dragons Hospitality Manager

Remember my brand-new, multi-million dollar, state-of-the-art rock climbing facility? Yeah, while managing that gym, I made some mistakes. Two of them involved hiring the wrong people for the wrong jobs.

First, I hired a Hospitality Manager—someone responsible for handling customer service, CRM systems, and managing the front desk staff.

One might assume this job would entail, I don't know...scheduling, staff check-ins, delegating cleaning tasks, etc.

Apparently, all of that was overlooked in the job description because the guy I hired thought his job was to create Dungeons and Dragons campaigns.

To be fair, he also created DnD characters, spent a lot of time Googling DnD lore, and assigned all of his staff as either "lawful good, chaotic good, lawful evil, or chaotic evil."

So, it's not like he was doing *completely* nothing.

I'm sure it was a huge staff morale boost to have your boss officially assign you as a *chaotic evil employee*. (I, unfortunately, never found out what my alignment was. Probably "overworked neutral.")

In case anyone is curious, I put him on a Performance Improvement Plan within two months of the facility opening.

*Mini Lesson: When staff start describing themselves as "chaotic good," dig deeper. If your employees are assigning themselves DnD alignments, it's worth checking whether they're doing their jobs... or just rolling dice.*

## The Program Manager Who Was "Working the Floor" (Aka Flirting with Clients)

While DnD battles were raging at the front desk, I had high hopes that my Program Manager was out there launching instructional programs, creating youth classes, and finding meaningful ways to connect with our clients.

She was not doing any of that.

Instead, she decided she needed to "work the floor" to better engage with clients.

Now, being the reasonable and *incredibly naïve* boss that I am, I approved her to "work the floor" as long as she was still developing programs.

Neither of those things happened.

Her version of *"working the floor"* was actually just flirting with clients.

(Yes, really.)

Meanwhile, while she was *"engaging with members"* (a phrase I now understand to be a red flag), her email inbox accumulated over 1,000 unread messages.

***Mini Lesson:*** *"Working the floor" should never mean avoiding real responsibilities. If someone uses vague language to justify not doing their job, start investigating.*

## Cleaning House: Firing My Entire Management Team

My gym opened in August.

By November, my Hospitality Manager was handed a severance package.

By February, my Program Manager was also let go.

Within three months, I let go of my entire management team.

My gym was barely five months old, and I had no one to run my largest departments.

So, I ran them.

And it sucked.

Honestly? I royally sucked at being a Program Manager, a Hospitality Manager, AND running the whole damn gym.

However, I managed to lay a very rough foundation for both departments, and I took my time to find and hire the right people.

As for my former Hospitality Manager? I later heard through the gossip-fueled grapevine that he's now working at a DnD shop.

I like to think that job is a better fit for him.

And my former Program Manager? I have no idea where she ended up, but I still have nightmares about her inbox.

The thing about firing someone is that it doesn't immediately exorcise their ghost.
Their mess still lingers. Their mistakes still haunt you.
You'll find their fingerprints on broken systems months after they're gone.
You'll stumble across half-finished projects, awkwardly

worded emails, and wildly inconsistent policies—and you'll have no idea why they were done that way, but now it's *your* job to fix it.

Their former staff? Still comparing everything you do to the way *they* did it.

Their bad habits? Infected the culture, and you're the one stuck detoxing the team.

Firing them ends their employment.

But the real cleanup? That takes *so* much longer.

### *Mini Lesson:*

*You're not just managing people—you're managing their ghosts.*
*The chaos they left behind.*
*The decisions they made that haunt your inbox.*
*The policies they created with zero logic.*
*You're not just leading the living—you're cleaning up after the administrative dead.*

## Detective Nikki & The 6 AM Yoga Demon

Because playing the roles of Hospitality Manager and Program Manager wasn't enough, I—at some point—also became a private investigator.

(You think I'm joking.)

Our gym offered a 6 AM sunrise yoga class, which may sound awful to some of you, but let me tell you—the yogis who attended this specific class were the most dedicated early risers I've ever seen.

Cult-level dedication.

They arrived in silence.
They rolled out their mats in eerie synchronicity.
They moved through sun salutations like a single, synchronized entity.

And their instructor?

Wasn't there. She was...a literal ghost.

One day, a desk staffer came to me and said:
*"Hey, uh...the 6 AM instructor hasn't been showing up for class."*

Which was odd because—since I was playing the role of GM and Hospitality Manager at the same time—I knew she was clocking in and out.

And yet, she wasn't there teaching the class.


## *The Investigation Begins*

Enter Private Investigator Nikki.

I checked the security footage.

No instructor.

But hilariously, the 6 AM yogis were still there.

Still rolling out their mats.
Still moving through an instructor-less practice.
Still doing the work their leader had abandoned.

Like a phantom cult, untethered from time, continuing their sacred rituals despite the absence of their supposed guide.

I had enough evidence to fire her—time theft is not tolerated.

But did I stop there?

No, of course not.

Because I'm an idiot, I woke up at 5 AM, dragged my overworked and underpaid ass to the gym, and showed up to the next 6 AM yoga class in person.

And guess what?

The instructor did not show up.

But the yogis did.

And yes—I joined them.

I, a non-yogi, fully integrated myself into The Cult of 6 AM.

And to this day, their eerie discipline haunts me.

Even without an instructor, they persisted.

Because their leader was never the instructor.

The cult had transcended the need for a guide.

Or, to put it less poetically, they were more dedicated than the person I was paying to be there.

So after my first and last sunrise yoga practice, I fired the instructor and updated my résumé to include:
-Paranormal cult observer
-Sherlock-level detective skills


## ***The Real Horror Story Begins***

Firing her should have been the end of it.

It was not.

Because the instructor refused to accept that she had ever been absent.

Even after being confronted with clear-cut security footage evidence, she insisted:

"I was there. I was always there."

Ma'am.

No, you were not.

At this point, I was convinced she was a demon.

Because she did not stop at mere gaslighting.

After her termination, she went full exorcist mode—sending me harassing emails telling me to go fuck myself, calling me a terrible human, and demanding that I admit she was never missing.

HR had to step in and directly tell her to stop contacting me.

Only then—only after an actual HR intervention—did the haunting finally end.

At least, I think it ended.

(I blocked her email address, so honestly maybe she's still been telling me to go fuck myself this entire time).

But one thing is certain—I had a dedicated community who genuinely *wanted* to be there at 6 AM (for whatever ungodly or otherworldly reason), and an instructor who *lied* about being there and quite literally ghosted her students.

Obviously, this wasn't fair to my clients. And like any good horror story...

That demon was exorcised.

*Mini Lesson: Just because someone's clocking in doesn't mean they're working. Trust, but verify—especially if something feels off. Security footage is your friend.*

## Zack, The Employee Who Fired Himself

Now, in case you missed it, the fun little motif of this chapter is that I've fired a lot of people.

But let me tell you about the one time an employee beat me to the punch and fired himself.

Zack. Oh, Zack.

Sometimes, in management, you create policies to ensure clarity and consistency among employees.

Sometimes, you accidentally hire the exact kind of person who will exploit every single loophole in those policies just to see how much they can get away with.

That was Zack.

Unfortunately for him, I have three higher education degrees in policy development and implementation.

Zack did not know that little fact about me.

At our gym, we had a very clear scheduling system:
Schedules were posted two weeks in advance.

If you needed time off, you put your availability in BEFORE the schedule was posted.

If you needed a shift covered after the schedule was posted, it was your responsibility to find a replacement.

It's a simple system. It worked.

Unless, of course, you're Zack.

Because Zack's favorite hobby was marking himself as unavailable AFTER the schedule was posted and then swearing up and down that he had done it beforehand.

The joke was on him because our scheduling platform automatically time-stamped every availability change.

And every single time, without fail, Zack changed his availability AFTER the schedule went live.

Which meant he was lying. Every. Single. Time.

But Zack was committed to the bit.

And sometimes, he would actually find shift coverage.

But other times, he wouldn't. And when he didn't, he'd come up with some absolute sob story about why he *couldn't possibly* work his shift.

Like clockwork.

One week? A sudden mystery illness.

The next? A family tragedy.

At one point, he even tried to tell me his childhood pet died.

Now, I'm not a monster. I take family emergencies seriously. I take illness seriously.

However, at a certain point, if someone's great-aunt's hamster keeps dying every two weeks, you start to notice a pattern.

### *The Final Straw*

Zack had already received two official write-ups for manipulating his schedule.

And one more scheduling offense meant termination.

So, when he (once again) changed his availability after the schedule was posted, I emailed him immediately and said:

*"Hey, Zack, just a reminder—this is your responsibility to fix. Please find shift coverage."*

He did not respond.

Until three hours before his shift.

And when he did, he sent me this absolute masterpiece of an email:

"Hello Nikki,
I understand that my inability to work today's shift will result in my termination, so I've decided to resign, effective immediately."

Zack literally fired himself.

I had already planned for him not to show up. I already had backup coverage.

But the fact that he preemptively quit before I could fire him?

That almost—almost—earned my respect.

## *The Real Punchline: Zack's Next Job*

Now, you'd think this is where Zack's story ends.

But somehow, it gets better.

Because, a few weeks later, he listed me as a reference for his next job.

I need you to really let that sink in.

The guy who spent months lying, dodging shifts, and actively working against my scheduling policies thought it was a good idea to put me on his résumé.

I do not know what he expected me to say.

But I do know exactly what I said when his potential new employer called.

And let's just say—Zack did not get the job.

Zack's resignation was a gift. His ghost was finally gone. But just when I thought I was free—there he was, haunting my inbox from beyond the managerial grave, asking me to be his reference. Some ghosts just refuse to stay dead.

*Mini Lesson: Sometimes, people fire themselves—and that's okay. Let them. Seriously.*

## The Poop-Colored Silver Lining of Hiring and Firing

**1.) Bad hires haunt more than your budget—they tank morale.** After I let Zach go, staff morale increased overnight. People don't just notice lazy coworkers—they resent them. Letting them go sends a powerful message that accountability matters.

**2.) You're not failing when you fire someone—you're fixing.** My gym was better without the DnD campaigns and flirt-fueled floor shifts. It didn't feel like progress in the moment, but it was.

**3.) Some ghosts of bad hires stick around longer than you want—but they teach you how to do better.** Hiring mistakes build future hiring wisdom. That's how I created tighter policies, asked better interview questions, and finally found people who gave a damn.

The ghosts of bad employees past will always linger. Their mistakes live on in the policies you create to prevent future disasters. Their stories will be passed down like managerial campfire horror stories. But the beauty of leadership is that, eventually, the ghosts fade—and the lessons they leave behind make you a stronger, sharper, and slightly more exhausted manager.

# | 4 |

# The Corporate Circus of Bullshit

## WHERE EVERY MEETING IS A THREE-RING DISASTER

Welcome to the show, folks!

Have you ever worked for a company that asks you to set goals for yourself?

I have.

It's the biggest load of airy fairy bullshit.

Why? Because goal-setting in corporate America is the equivalent of a trained poodle act.

- Jump through this hoop.

- Stand on your hind legs.

- Perform an elaborate trick for the approval of your boss.

But here's the thing:

What if your boss doesn't care about your goals? Then the entire exercise was just that—an exercise. A performative little show where management gets to pretend they care about development while actually doing nothing.

And the real kicker? If your boss decides your goals aren't "aligned" with their mysterious, ever-shifting priorities—priorities they never actually communicated to you—then you just wasted all that time and effort for nothing.
No feedback. No guidance. No follow-through.
Just *poof!* Into the corporate ether, your ideas go.

That's the thing about corporate leadership.
It's not about making decisions.
It's about creating the illusion that decisions are being made.

And if you're smart enough to recognize that? Congratulations.
You just got cast in the role of 'Managing Up'—whether you wanted the part or not.

## ACT ONE: The Monster Truck Debate

In management, you often have to advocate for your staff. Usually, that means ensuring they get fair treatment, proper schedules, and reasonable pay.

Occasionally, however, it means stepping into the center ring of a full-blown managerial circus and juggling flaming nonsense while corporate acrobats leap through hoops of illogical decision-making.

Example?
A snowstorm.

The entire town was shut down. Schools? Closed. Businesses? Closed. The roads? Absolutely buried in snow. I knew, without a doubt, that we needed to close early to keep my staff and clients safe. It was an obvious call. Or at least, it should have been.

Instead of making the logical choice, my boss at the time decided this was the perfect moment for a philosophical conversation about whether or not my desk staff might drive monster trucks.

Yes. Monster trucks.

Because, and I quote, "Some of them might own one and be able to get to work, right? We can't assume they all drive normal cars."

As I sat there, slowly losing my will to live, my boss continued to spiral into an over-analysis of potential solutions to get staff to work.

- Could we push back the schedule so our employees could drive behind the snowplows?
  *(I don't manage the snowplows. Nor do I know their routes or their estimated times of arrival.)*
- Could we stagger shifts so that only the most 'snow-ready' employees come in?
- Should we poll the staff to see if anyone has a lifted truck or chains on their tires?

I wish I were making this up.

Meanwhile, outside our building, literal blizzard conditions were unfolding. The kind of snowstorm where you can barely see two feet in front of you. Where stepping outside feels like entering a frozen hellscape.

And yet, I engaged in a never-ending discussion about monster trucks.

Eventually, after an exhausting back-and-forth, I laid it out as plainly as I could:

"If we're the only business still open while the city's under a blizzard warning, and someone gets hurt trying to drive here—especially after we handpicked the 'most snow-ready' staff to come in—it's going to look real bad. Not just morally, but legally. It's negligent at best, and a PR disaster at worst."

That was the moment it clicked.

Not because he didn't care about employee safety—he did—but because the way I framed it finally aligned with how he processes risk: not just in terms of logistics, but liability. Once he realized it was in the best interest of the *business* to close, that's when the plan got his full support.

And just like that, we closed early.

But what did I learn?

**Lesson #1:** Some managers will overcomplicate the simplest of decisions.
You can present clear evidence that something is the right call, and they'll still want to discuss hypothetical edge cases that do not matter.

**Lesson #2:** Sometimes, you have to manage up, sideways, and diagonally just to get a decision made.
I was managing my boss's indecision, my staff's expectations, and Mother Nature's complete disregard for my stress levels.

**Lesson #3:** The bigger the storm, the more convoluted the decision-making process becomes.

Whether it's a blizzard, a staffing crisis, or a budget meeting, certain managers will find ways to make the most obvious decisions wildly difficult.

Would it have been easier if my staff actually drove monster trucks? Maybe.

Would I have rather taken my chances out in the snowstorm than sit through a conversation about hypothetical monster trucks?

Absolutely.

---

# ACT TWO: Jumping Through Hoops for "Growth"

---

*(Or: The Greatest Show of Corporate Clownery)*

Welcome to the Big Top of Bullshit, where your career development is a dazzling illusion, and your company's leadership is just a bunch of clowns in suits.

Managers with a corporate mindset love to use meaningless buzzwords to make your career path seem vibrant, strategic, and fulfilling.

This is a smoke-and-mirrors act designed to make you believe you have growth opportunities when, in reality, you are simply a circus performer being asked to jump through arbitrary hoops for absolutely no reward.

## *Act 2 Part 1: The Lingo of Smoke and Mirrors*

The corporate world has its own scripted language, a lexicon of absolute nonsense designed to confuse, obfuscate, and make very simple things sound complex and important.

### Corporate Buzzword Bingo (A.K.A. The Greatest Scam Ever Performed)

- **Low-hanging fruit** → (a.k.a. *"Do the easy thing first, but act like it's an achievement."*)
- **Circle back** → (*"I don't want to deal with this right now, and I hope you forget about it."*)
- **Synergy** → (*"Collaboration, but make it sound expensive."*)
- **Leverage** → (*"Use something, but in a way that makes me sound like a thought leader."*)
- **Deep dive** → (*"Look into this more because I didn't understand it the first time."*)
- **Move the needle** → (*"Make progress, but pretend it's groundbreaking."*)
- **Ideate** → (*"Brainstorm, but with a master's degree."*)
- **Let's double-click on that** → (*"Let's discuss it, but in a way that makes me feel tech-savvy."*)
- **Net-net** → (*"The bottom line, but with extra syllables to waste your time."*)

- **At the end of the day** → (*Usually followed by nonsense that adds no value whatsoever*).

## Corporate Smoke & Mirrors Tricks

- **Bandwidth** → (*"I don't have time for this, but I don't want to say that out loud."*)
- **Paradigm shift** → (*"We changed something and want to sound revolutionary about it."*)
- **Pivot** → (*"We had no plan, and now we need a new one."*)
- **Disruptor/Disruptive** → (*"Not actually disruptive at all, just marketing fluff."*)
- **Thought leader** → (*"Self-proclaimed. No one actually calls them this."*)
- **Results-driven** → (*"As opposed to...failing on purpose?"*)
- **Actionable insights** → (*"Just say 'useful information,' Chad."*)
- **Table that** → (*"We will never speak of this again."*)
- **Let's take this offline** → (*"This meeting should have been an email."*)

## Fake Motivation / Corporate Gaslighting (The Emotional Manipulation Act!)

- **We're like a family** → (*Red flag! You are not a family. You are underpaid colleagues who make passive-aggressive small talk at the Keurig machine.*)
- **Give 110%** → (*Mathematically impossible. Also, no.*)
- **Fail fast, fail often** → (*Why are we encouraging failure?*)

- **Work hard, play hard** → (*Translation: "You'll work 60-hour weeks, and we'll buy you pizza once a quarter."*)
- **Hustle culture** → (*See above, but now with burnout!*)
- **Open-door policy** → (*Until you actually complain, then the door is metaphorically slammed shut.*)
- **Wear multiple hats** → (*You're about to do three people's jobs for the price of one.*)
- **Take ownership** → (*We will not be giving you a raise.*)
- **Proactive, not reactive** → (*We will give you zero direction but expect you to read minds.*)
- **Do more with less** → (*Get ready to be underpaid and overworked.*)
- **Aligned on this?** → (*Please just agree with me so we can end this call.*)

### And, of course, corporate email nonsense:

- **Per my last email** → (*Did you even read what I wrote?*)
- **Just following up** → (*I know you ignored me the first time.*)
- **To piggyback off that** → (*I have nothing new to add, but I want to speak.*)
- **Hope this finds you well** → (*This email is about to ruin your day.*)
- **Looping in [Name]** → (*I'm done dealing with this. You handle it now.*)

## Lesson #1: It's All Just Airy Fairy Bullshit.

Corporate jargon is a smoke-and-mirrors trick. It makes

simple things sound complicated so that no one realizes they're doing a whole lot of nothing.

## Act 2 Part 2: The Quarterly Review Tightrope

Corporate leadership loves to pretend they care about your professional development—so much so that they ask employees to self-review at the end of each quarter and then create three goals for the next quarter.
This is the motherload of Airy Fairy Bullshit.

Why?
Because no one actually cares about your goals.

- Lazy, incompetent employees? → They set bullshit goals, accomplish nothing, and continue being lazy and incompetent.
- Ambitious employees? → They put actual thought and effort into strategic goals...only to be ignored.

I, stupidly, made the mistake one quarter of setting genuinely ambitious goals—goals that, if achieved, would make a difference company-wide.

I sent a beautifully crafted email to my boss highlighting my goals and why I felt they would help make a meaningful contribution to the company.

- **Goal #1**: Editing the company website to remove glaring spelling errors in the hero section. (Because I'd rather not work for a business that doesn't know the difference between "your" and "you're ".)

- **Goal #2**: Drafting a monthly newsletter to keep clients informed and engaged.
- **Goal #3**: Standardize company-wide policies to improve consistency.

I was genuinely excited. I thought these goals would actually matter.

Do you know what my boss said?

Nothing.
Radio silence.
Not even an acknowledgment that he saw the email.

Several weeks later, I brought them up in a meeting.
His response?

"Oh! Yeah. Those are...interesting. But instead of that, have you considered...increasing membership sales?"

I stared at him.
I blinked.

I'm no expert here, my guy, but maybe—just MAYBE—if our website didn't look like it was written by an AI that failed third-grade grammar, we'd sell more memberships.

My boss proceeded to hand me the ultimate platter of corporate buzzwords:

"Yeah, so, let's pivot with your goals to find some actionable items that will be a bit more results-driven. I propose we table the goals you originally presented and circle back to them next quarter. Does this sound like something we can be aligned on?"

I definitely got buzzword BINGO in that meeting.

**Lesson #2: Corporate Goal-Setting is Just a Circus Act.**
They don't actually want you to grow. They want to pretend they're fostering growth so they can tick a box and call it employee engagement. And they throw in some buzzwords to make it seem less bull-shitty.

## *Final Takeaway from Preforming in the Circus*

- You will jump through hoops that don't matter.
- You will be forced to watch corporate smoke-and-mirrors tricks.
- You will walk the tightrope of "growth" while getting absolutely nowhere.

And at the end of it all?

Your reward is…more hoop-jumping.

Welcome to the circus.

## INTERMISSION: The Big Top Act of Leadership Clown College

Once a year, the corporate circus packs up its tent and heads to Leadership Retreats, a magical place where executives gather to *ideate, synergize,* and *align on actionable insights*—or, more accurately, where they go to waste company money while pretending to be visionaries and drowning you in corporate buzzwords. (Leadership retreats are, however, the ultimate game of buzzword Bingo).

A leadership retreat is basically a summer camp for corporate nonsense, except instead of making friendship bracelets and learning archery, you're subjected to:

- **Trust falls and rope courses** (because I really love being in close proximity and touched by coworkers I barely know)

- **Keynote speeches full of misquoted inspiration** ("As Steve Jobs once said...wait, maybe it was Oprah?")

- **Breakout sessions that solve nothing** ("Let's circle back on that...after lunch...or never.")

- **The CEO getting weirdly emotional about company values** (which will be ignored by Monday)

- **A "team-building exercise" where they make you share a "fun fact" about yourself** (Corporate ice-breakers are psychological warfare)

- **An elaborate dinner where the execs get drunk and tell you how much they 'appreciate you'** (Right before they deny your budget request next quarter)

Meanwhile, all of your actual work is put on pause because while you're stuck making small talk with Barb from Finance, your inbox back at the office is slowly filling with 800 unread emails—a fresh hell you'll have to dig yourself out of on Monday.

And let's not forget the real trauma: the drunken confessions that will haunt you for life because the free alcohol at these things is a corporate trap. It lulls your colleagues into a false sense of emotional intimacy, which inevitably leads to Barb from Finance trauma-dumping all of her deepest regrets onto you.

So now, in addition to resenting leadership retreats, you now:

- Have a new and deeply uncomfortable understanding of Barb's third divorce

- Know way too much about Chad from Marketing's personal vendetta against Greg

- Can never look at Tom from IT the same way again after what he admitted about his past job

- Are behind on all your actual work because the retreat was a colossal waste of time

But hey! At least you got free alcohol.
Despite the fact that you'll now need therapy to process all the drunken things Barb from Finance confided in you about.

**Final takeaway?**
Leadership retreats are not about learning to lead.
They are about pretending to lead in a luxury resort while creating new workplace trauma.

Welcome to Leadership Clown College.

---

## FINAL ACT: The Clown Car That Is Corporate Decision-Making

---

You might be juggling the most, giving the best performance, and working the crowd perfectly, but the clowns barely holding the show together will still get promoted over you.

Welcome to the real final act—the one where the most unqualified performers get center stage while you're left sweeping up elephant shit behind the scenes.

The sad truth?
I have so many stories I could put in this section. It happens all the time.

Some bozo—who:

- Can't respond to emails

- Is always late to the Zoom meeting

- Spends half their day on "coffee chats" and LinkedIn posts

- And who you genuinely find yourself asking: *"What do they even DO during their work day?"*

Somehow gets promoted over you.

Because corporate decision-making makes absolutely no sense.

And honestly? I don't have a silver lining for this one.
It is infuriating.
It is exhausting.
It is demoralizing to continually feel overlooked, undervalued, and underpaid while watching human PowerPoint presentations rise through the ranks.

It's hard to sit in the bleachers watching the clowns balance motorcycles on their noses while swallowing fire and farting swords when you know damn well the act you proposed:

- Made more sense
- Was safer
- Would have sold more tickets
- And actually would have produced an even bigger 'wow' factor

But, alas—it is the clowns who get the standing ovation.

**Lesson #1: Corporate Promotions Are a Magic Trick**
(*Now you see logic, now you don't!*)

- The best person for the job? Rarely gets it.
- The most competent, reliable employee? Probably still stuck in their current role.
- The executive who spent the least amount of time actually doing any real work? *Welcome to the C-Suite.*

**Lesson #2: You Are Not in Control of the Big Show**
You can juggle flaming chainsaws and do backflips through hoops while managing your entire team flawlessly, but if leadership wants to promote the guy who once emailed a PDF to himself and called it "automation," there is nothing you can do about it.

## Lesson #3: It's Not About Talent—It's About Who Can Work the Crowd

And by *"work the crowd,"* I mean:

- Attend unnecessary meetings and call it "cross-functional collaboration"
- Speak exclusively in Corporate Smoke & Mirrors
- Give absolutely zero pushback when leadership suggests something dumb

Meanwhile, the people actually doing the work? They often *don't* get promoted—not because they're not qualified, but because they're too valuable where they are. Leadership doesn't want to lose the one person keeping things from falling apart. So instead, they promote someone they see as a "team player" with a "positive attitude" (read: someone who smiles a lot and doesn't rock the boat).

The result? Talented people stay stuck while the charismatic nonsense-peddlers rise.

At the end of the day, this is the corporate circus.
And unfortunately, the ringmaster isn't the one who actually knows how to run the show.

# The Poop-Colored Sawdust on the Circus Floor

## 1.) Managing Up Is an Unpaid Second Job

- You will learn to anticipate your boss's incompetence before they even realize there's a problem.
- You will learn to make decisions for them before they have a chance to derail the entire plan.
- You will learn to smile through the absurdity and not let it break your spirit. (*Most of the time.*)

## 2.) Corporate Goal-Setting Is a Scam Wrapped in Airy Fairy Buzzwords

- They don't want your ideas—they want you to pretend you're growing while standing still.
- They don't care about your ambitions—they care about whether or not they can slap a meaningless "Professional Development" badge on their HR reports.
- They don't actually want change—they want a list of initiatives they can ignore.

## 3.) The Greatest Trick Corporate Leadership Ever Pulled Was Convincing People They Lead Anything

- Leadership *should* mean guidance, accountability, and vision.

- But leadership actually means stalling for time in meetings and throwing around words like "synergy."
- They aren't making real decisions—they're just managing the illusion that they are.

**But here's the thing:**

The circus happening in the big ring above you will affect you.
The clowns in charge will make your life harder.
And the absolute, unrelenting chaos will make you want to rage quit at least once a week.

**It's your job not to let it affect your team.**

At the end of the day?
Your bosses might be actual clowns.
But that doesn't mean you have to be one, too.

Don't get distracted by the circus.
Run your goddamn team.

# | 5 |

# The Complaint Chronicles

## TALES OF BETRAYAL, DRAMA, AND 1-STAR REVIEWS

Hello and welcome to management, where every minor client inconvenience is treated like a catastrophic and unforeseen betrayal. And those petty client inconveniences are often, frequently, and almost always escalated to you.

I know we've all been taught that the customer is always right. I'm here to tell you that saying is absolute bullshit. When you work in any industry involving safety, health, risk management, or equipment, let me say this loud and clear: The customer is *not* always right. In fact, the staff you've trained almost certainly know more about the product they're selling than the customer does.

Great, with that disclaimer out of the way, please enjoy some painfully real situations where clients were wrong and blew the situation way out of proportion. Buckle up because this chapter is a soap opera of betrayal, scandal, and petty grievances—all starring our most dramatic supporting characters: clients who believe the world revolves around them.

## Episode 1: The Headlights Scandal of a Quiet Little Suburb

Up until this point, all of my stories have been summaries of incidents written from my (admittedly subjective) perspective. For this one, though, I'm just going to drop in the actual email that landed in my inbox—because there is no way I could summarize it better than how it was originally presented to me. (I am, of course, removing sensitive and personal details from these receipts.)

Some complaints are expected: billing issues, equipment malfunctions, the occasional rude customer service interaction. And then...there are complaints like this:

**Subject:** Ongoing Issue with Headlights in Your Parking Lot
**To:** Nikki

*Hello, PIC,*

I am a resident of the apartment complex next door to your facility, and I have been noticing a recurring issue. Every evening, between 9 PM and 11 PM or later, I observe a black Nissan car parked in your lot with its headlights on. Considering the time, it appears to be associated with your staff, possibly someone picking up your member.

As my apartment directly faces the parking area, the headlights shining into our windows at night have become quite disruptive. This car is always parked at the lot very near to the entrance. I kindly ask if you could remind your staff to refrain from leaving the headlights on while parked or to park in a way that avoids shining lights into residential windows.

If this issue continues, I may need to involve the apartment management and, if necessary, consult with local authorities. I trust that this can be resolved amicably, and I appreciate your understanding and cooperation in advance.

*Thank you for your attention to this matter.*

Yeah, it's a *public* parking lot...that I do not manage, nor do I have control over who comes or goes.

My response was as follows:

**Subject:** RE: Ongoing Issue with Headlights in Your Parking Lot
**To:** [Redacted]

Hello,

Thank you for reaching out and bringing this to our attention. I understand how frustrating it can be to have bright headlights shining into your apartment late at night.

That said, our parking lot is publicly accessible and is also shared with the businesses next door, meaning we do not have control over who parks there or how long they leave their headlights on. While I can certainly remind our staff to be mindful of this, I cannot guarantee that the vehicle in question belongs to an employee or member.

If this continues to be a concern, I'd recommend reaching out to your apartment management to discuss potential solutions, such as window coverings or window film to mitigate light, as we do not have jurisdiction over the lot's use.

I appreciate your understanding, and please let me know if there's anything else I can do on my end.

I also took the liberty of drafting an additional email for them since, apparently, curtains were not a viable option:

**Subject:** Excessive Lunar Glow Disrupting My Sleep
**To:** NASA, The Moon, and Whoever Controls the Night Sky

Dear NASA,

I am a resident of an apartment complex, and I have noticed a recurring issue. Every evening, between 9 PM and 11 PM or later, I observed an extremely bright celestial object in the sky. The light it emits is disruptive to my sleep, and I kindly ask if you could adjust its brightness or reposition it elsewhere.

If this issue continues, I may need to involve my apartment management and, if necessary, consult with local authorities.

Best regards,
*The Same Person Who Complained About Headlights in a Public Parking Lot*

Lesson Learned: You are not in charge of the moon, the parking lot, or other people's unreasonable expectations. Know where your responsibility ends—and don't let people drag you into drama you don't own.

...Will the headlights return? Will the apartment complex rise in defiance? Will NASA finally respond to the excessive brightness of the moon? *Tune in next time for another thrilling episode of The Complaint Chronicles.*

## Episode 2: The Wrath of the 1-Star Neighbor

At one point, I lived stupidly close to the gym I was managing. I'm talking a seven-minute drive—just two miles away from my workplace.

One of my neighbors, whom we'll call *Vance*, was a little too excited when he discovered that the person running his favorite gym lived on his street. Every time I walked my dogs, he would go out of his way to stop me and talk about the gym.

Honestly? At first, it was fine. It was even nice—having someone in my neighborhood who was excited about the gym and singing its praises to everyone he knew. Free word-of-mouth marketing? Sure, I'll take it.

Until one fateful day when Vance showed up at the gym, demanding to speak with me.

My desk staff, doing their job, let him know that I was tied up in meetings but encouraged him to email me so we could schedule a time to chat.

Vance's response?
A full-blown tantrum.

No joke—he got angry and rude with my staff because *I* had the audacity to have a prior obligation.

Then, he did what any mature, rational adult would do: he took to the internet to exact his revenge.

Vance left a 1-star Google review about how horrible I was for *being in a meeting* and *not immediately dropping everything to talk to him.*

Friendly reminder: this man was my neighbor. He saw me all the time.
At literally any point, he could have asked me his question when we crossed paths.

What Was So Urgent?

Was it an emergency? A serious safety issue? A gym catastrophe?

No.
He wanted to book a group event.

That's it.

Something that could be booked on our website.
Something that had nothing to do with me.
Something that he literally could have done himself without speaking to anyone.

Instead, he threw a fit, was rude to my staff, and left a 1-star review.

All because I was in a meeting.


## *Petty Revenge, Neighborhood Edition*

Now, this next part?
This is where the story gets good.

The very next day, my neighborhood hosted a block party.

Oh, and you better believe I told everyone about our 1-star neighbor.

I casually mentioned how he'd left a petty, dramatic review, how he treated my staff poorly, and how he threw a literal tantrum in my gym over something he could have done online in 30 seconds.

And just like that, Vance's reputation was sealed.

Now? He is forever known as "The 1-Star Neighbor."
(Sorry, not sorry, Vance.)

### *The Aftermath*

To this day, Vance remains the guy who fumbled a perfectly good neighborly relationship in exchange for a petty online review.

Was it worth it? Only the Google algorithm knows.

(Oh, and in case you're wondering, he *did* eventually remove his review. Probably around the time the entire neighborhood started shunning him.)

We still passed each other on the street from time to time. He'd give me awkward nods, and I'd respond with the kind of smile you give someone who once tried to ruin your job because they had to wait five minutes. We never actually spoke again, and honestly? That was for the best.

### Final Lessons From Vance's Temper Tantrum?

1. **Set boundaries between work and home.**
   If you live close to your workplace and are *painfully* ingrained in your community, set hard and firm boundaries. Otherwise, some entitled weirdo will show up at your job and expect you to cater to them.
2. **People will absolutely ruin their own reputations.**
   Vance chose violence. Vance faced consequences. And I never had to lift a finger.
3. **Petty people will be petty—but sometimes, the universe serves justice.**

In the end, Vance got exactly what he gave. A taste of his own pettiness.

## Episode 3: Karen's Dramatic Exit (A Story of Unnecessary Racism and Refunded Regrets)

And now, to close out our drama-filled soap opera of client complaints, I present to you the worst interaction I've ever had in any customer-facing role.

### *The Racist Homeschool Mom*

One day, while running a gym, I had the privilege of hosting a school group from the South Side of Chicago.

Most of these kids had never climbed before.
They were excited, fearless, and having an absolute blast.
It was exactly the kind of experience I love to see in the gym.

At the same time, we also had a homeschool group from the North Side of Chicago booked.

For those unfamiliar with Chicagoland demographics, let me spell it out:
One of these groups was primarily black.
One of these groups was primarily white.

I'll let you guess which one was which.

## Karen Enters the Chat

At some point, a homeschool mom—we'll call her Karen—stormed up to the front desk.

I, being the unshakeable rock of a manager that I am, stepped in to de-escalate the situation.

Karen, red in the face, turned to me and hissed:
*"I can't believe you let those kind of people in here!"*

Now, at this moment, I had no idea what she was talking about.
(Overworked and underpaid squirrel brain, remember?)

So, being the reasonable and fact-based person that I am, I asked:
*"Who are you referring to?"*

Karen, still fuming, gestured toward the school kids.

I—*still not comprehending that I was speaking to a racist lunatic*—responded with:
*"Oh, public school kids? Yeah, we work with a lot of different schools."*

Big mistake.

Because this was the moment Karen *lost* it.

*"NO! THE BLACK PEOPLE!"*

Ah. There it was.
The moment my brain finally clicked into "Oh, we're dealing with a racist today."

I took a deep breath.

Looked her dead in the eyes.

And calmly said:
*"Ma'am, all I see are kids having fun and not bothering anyone else. I am kindly going to issue you a refund and ask you to leave."*

Luckily, she was already halfway out the door—because gods forbid she share the same air as different races, ethnicities, or ideologies.

My Only Regret?

I refunded her.
I wish I hadn't.

**Final Lessons from Karen:**

1. **Don't refund racists.**
   Let them lose their money and their dignity in one fell swoop.
2. **People are REALLY stupid.**
   Like, *staggeringly, embarrassingly* stupid.
3. **Sometimes, your job isn't just customer service—it's protecting your space from people**

**who don't deserve to be in it.**

Karen walked in thinking she could throw a tantrum and be validated.

Karen left, knowing she was absolutely not welcome.

And that?

That is how you handle a Karen.

## The Poop-Colored Silver Lining of The Complaint Chronicles

1. **Some People Will Complain About Anything—And That's Not Your Problem.**

   If someone is determined to be miserable, *they will find a way.* You could hand them a free membership, carry them up the climbing wall yourself, and send them home with a gift basket—and they'd still leave a 1-star review because the gift basket didn't have their preferred brand of crackers. Accept it. Let it roll off your back.

2. **Your Petty Clients Will Live in Infamy—And That's Kind of Beautiful.**

   Vance the 1-star neighbor? His reputation is *forever* sealed in my neighborhood. Karen the racist? She got publicly refunded and booted, her tantrum serving only to make me look like the hero in my own story.

The parking lot email guy? He will forever be the person who threatened to involve *law enforcement* over headlights in a *public* parking lot. Sometimes, the best revenge is letting these people's own absurdity be the thing that defines them.

3. **You Can't Control the Complaints—But You *Can* Control the Clapbacks.**

    At the end of the day, you're not obligated to bend over backward for people who mistake customer service for personal servitude. The power move? Respond professionally, stand firm in reality, and—when appropriate—weaponize just enough sarcasm to make their ridiculousness *painfully* clear.

And with that, we close another episode of the Complaint Chronicles. Tune in next week when a customer threatens legal action over a completely normal and non-controversial gym policy.

# | 6 |

# Welcome to the Boys' Club

## A MASTERCLASS IN MALE-DOMI-NATED MADNESS

If you identify as a female and you've ever worked in a male-dominated industry, congratulations! You've probably developed a high tolerance for bullshit, a mental archive of the most absurdly sexist things ever said to you, and a deep appreciation for the rare competent men who actually just do their jobs without treating you like an alien species.

I'd love to tell you that being a woman in leadership has been a rewarding and fulfilling journey, but mostly, it's been a bizarre mix of:

- Being ignored, interrupted, or dismissed in meetings, only to have a man repeat the same thing I just said—and get praised for it. (More often than not, the man in question also happens to be my boss.)

- Being asked to prove my competence in ways my male counterparts never had to.
- Being mansplained by men who had *less* experience, *less* knowledge, and *less* common sense than a damp paper towel.
- And, of course, getting hit on in completely inappropriate workplace scenarios—because what's professional development without a side of unsolicited flirting?

This chapter is dedicated to all the women who have ever had to be five times more competent just to be taken half as seriously. To the ones who kept their cool when a man explained their own job to them. To the women who walked into work every day knowing that the biggest challenge wasn't the job itself but the fragile egos of the men around them.

What's more, this sort of sexist bullshit doesn't just come from colleagues across your industry. No, the clients and customers you serve also treat you differently because you don't "look the part" of a boss.

Let's get into it.

## The Time I Had to Teach a "Professional" Electrician How to Use a Lift

I once had to teach a self-proclaimed professional electrician how to operate a boom lift.

Let's pause here.
Let's all take a moment to reflect.

Because if there's one thing I, a facility manager, should never have to do, it's teach the person I hired for a job how to use the equipment to do the job I hired them for.

But, alas, there I was.

This man had assured me he could operate any lift. He'd worked with lifts his entire career. This was his area of expertise.

And yet, when the time came to actually use the lift, he just...stood there.

> **Me:** "Okay, go ahead and turn it on."
> **Electrician:** *"How?"*
> **Me:** "You said you've operated NiftyLifts before?"
> **Electrician:** *"Yeah, yeah, I just...uh...this one looks a little different."*
> **Me:** *Literally turns the key.* "It's the same as every other

lift."

**Electrician:** *"Oh! Yeah! Haha, that's right. Got it now."*

Sir.

I walked away from that situation with two conclusions:

> 1.) I know more about boom lifts than a trained professional, which is both impressive and deeply concerning.
>
> 2.) If a woman ever admitted to not knowing how to use a basic piece of equipment after claiming she was an expert, she'd be immediately deemed incompetent and never trusted again. Meanwhile, this guy? Just a little 'confused' for a moment. A 'little rusty.' A 'quick learner.'

If the roles had been reversed—if I had stared at that lift with the same blank expression and asked how to turn it on—my credibility would have evaporated on the spot. I would've been deemed unqualified, written off as a token hire, and my leadership questioned. But this guy? He got a chuckle and a "No worries, bro." That's the luxury of being a man in a male-dominated industry: your mistakes are forgiven. Women don't get that kind of grace. We get one shot to be flawless—or we're never trusted again.

But oh, it gets worse.

Because after I helped him, he had the audacity to turn to me and say:

*"Wow, NiftyLift should use you for a slogan! So easy to use, even a woman can do it!"*

Excuse me, sir, would you like to be thrown off the lift?

(PSA to NiftyLift: I could not possibly be more uninterested in being your spokesperson for women who operate heavy machinery. Please do not use me as a slogan.)

**Lesson Learned?**
If you ever doubt your own competence in a male-dominated field, just remember: a fully grown man once fumbled a boom lift so badly that I, a completely unrelated professional, had to teach him how to use it.

## The Dancing Incident *(Or: The Unfortunate Reality of Being a Woman in Fitness & Sports)*

I dance.

Not professionally. Not for an audience. Just as a fitness hobby that I enjoy because it's fun, incredibly difficult, and a great workout.

Men, however, do not understand this concept.

Every single time a man learns that I dance, the conversation immediately goes off the rails.

Examples include:

- **"Ohhh, do you do private shows?"** (Disgusting. Immediately, no.)
- **"Damn, can I come watch sometime?"** (Absolutely not.)
- **"I'd love a one-on-one lesson ;)"** (You'd love a swift kick to the shin, too.)
- **"I bet you're really flexible, huh?"** (I bet you've never satisfied a woman in your life.)

The wildest part? These comments don't come from random men in bars.
They come from co-workers. Industry professionals. Colleagues who should know better.

These comments aren't just tone-deaf—they're a reflection of how women in fitness are so often reduced to our bodies, no matter how skilled or knowledgeable we are. A male athlete can wear compression shorts and deadlift 300 pounds, and no one sexualizes it. A woman climbs, dances, or trains with any kind of grace or strength, and suddenly it's an invitation for commentary. It's not admiration—it's objectification disguised as banter. And it's exhausting.

Would I ever ask a male coworker if I could come watch him deadlift in his garage? No. That would be wildly inappropriate.

But that's the thing about being a woman in the fitness industry.

Your competence is questioned, but your body is fair game for commentary.

**Lesson learned?**
If you tell a man you dance, be prepared for him to lose every last brain cell he has.

---

## Clients Who Assume I Am Not The Manager

---

Welcome to another episode of **"Men Underestimating Women in Leadership,"** where I, the actual manager, will be told repeatedly that I cannot possibly be the manager.

The script is always the same:

1.) Customer (usually male) asks to speak with the manager.
2.) I step out.
3.) Customer looks me up and down. Blinks. Hesitates.
4.) Customer says some variation of, "Oh. I asked for the manager."
5.) I stare at them, deadpan, before responding, "That's me."
6.) Customer processes this information like malfunctioning robots before reluctantly continuing their complaint.

It's a pattern so predictable that at this point, I could set it to music.

## *ACT ONE: The Equipment Guy Who Wanted a "Real Manager"*

One of my favorite incidents happened when an outside vendor came in to service some of our equipment. He walked up to the front desk, asked to speak with the manager, and I—doing my job—walked out to meet him.

He took one look at me and went:
*"Oh. I meant the manager."*

Buddy. What the hell do you think I am? A hologram?

So I just smiled, nodded, and said, *"And here I am. What do you need?"*

The man visibly struggled to accept reality. His eyes darted around the gym, probably hoping a 6'3" guy in a Patagonia vest would emerge and save him from this nightmare of having to talk to a woman in charge.

Eventually, he begrudgingly accepted my existence and continued his work. But he did so with the deep discomfort of a man who felt the natural order of the universe had been disrupted.

### ACT TWO: "Do You Need to Call Your Boss?"

Ah, yes. The *other* classic. The moment when, after realizing that yes, I am indeed the manager, a man still refuses to believe I hold actual decision-making power.

This usually happens when a male customer or contractor has a request that they assume will require "higher-up approval."

*"Can you adjust the pricing?"*
*"Can you make an exception for me?"*
*"Can you change this gym policy just for me?"*

And when I say no—because it is my call to make—they hit me with the dreaded:
*"Well, do you need to call your boss?"*

Sir.
I am the final boss.
If there was a super-secret higher-up manager hiding in the back, trust me, I would have called them out to deal with you already.

But no. You are stuck with me. And my answer is still no.

### ACT THREE: "Oh, I Thought You Were Just Front Desk."

This one's always a fun surprise—when someone assumes you're "just" an entry-level employee because they cannot compute that you run the entire facility.

Now, let's get something straight: There is absolutely nothing wrong with being front desk staff. The people working the front desk? They know more than you. They have more patience than you. And they are absolutely the last people you want to piss off because they know exactly how to make your life difficult without breaking a single rule.

So, when a customer once walked up to me, scoffed and said, *"I don't need help checking in—I need the manager,"* I simply smiled and responded, *"Good news! You found her!"*

And the look of absolute regret that washed over his face? Delicious.

## The Poop-Colored Silver Lining of Working in a Boys' Club

1. **You Will Be Underestimated.**
   And then? You will prove them wrong. Again. And again. And again.
2. **You Will Have to Work Twice as Hard.**
   Not because you're less capable, but because the default assumption is that you are less capable. So, you'll constantly have to prove yourself while men fumble their way through their jobs with confidence.
3. **You Will Learn How to Navigate Absolute Nonsense with Unshakable Grace.**

Men will tell on themselves. Constantly.

They will reveal their incompetence. They will say things that make no sense. They will openly admit they don't know how to do something they *claimed* to be experts at. And yet, they will still believe they deserve to be in charge.

And at the end of the day?

**You don't actually have to change the boys' club. You just have to be so good at your job that their opinions stop mattering.**

I hate that this chapter even needs to exist.

I've always promised myself that I would never cry *sexism* when I didn't get a job. I swore I'd never play the gender card, never let being a woman in leadership define my experiences, and never let it become an excuse.

But here's the thing: **this chapter isn't an excuse. It's a fact.**

The boys' club is **real.** The double standards are **real.**

And no matter how hard I work, no matter how much I prove myself, I know there will always be men who look at me and assume I *can't* possibly be in charge.

That's why this chapter exists. Not because I want to write about sexism, but because it would be dishonest *not to.*

# | 7 |

# Navigating Your Boss's Inefficiencies

## A ROAD MAP THROUGH MANAGERIAL MAYHEM

*O**r: How to Get Shit Done When Leadership is Useless*

If you're lucky, your boss is competent, responsive, and organized.
I am not lucky.

In my years of management, I've had bosses who can't make a decision, bosses who pretend they know what they're doing when they absolutely do not, and bosses who just...disappear when things get hard.

What I've learned?
You cannot rely on leadership to lead.

If you want things done, you have to navigate around their incompetence and find your own path forward. And, most importantly, do what's right for YOUR team—even if it means going completely off-road while your bosses are doing donuts around nonsensical ideas.

So, let me take you on a road trip through the scenic landscapes of managerial nonsense—complete with detours, roadblocks, and emergency U-turns.

Buckle up. The road gets bumpy.

## ROADBLOCK #1: Lost in the Corporate Wilderness - The Case of the Missing Google Form

*(Or: How Asking for a Simple Link Became a Multi-Day Scavenger Hunt)*

There are many things in life that should be easy. Finding a Google Form should be one of them.

And yet, in the world of corporate inefficiency, even the simplest request can turn into an Oregon Trail-style expedition—complete with unnecessary detours, unexpected roadblocks, and the creeping realization that you may never reach your destination.

Let me take you on a journey.

## STEP 1: THE NAVIGATION FAIL

One day, I received the following email from my boss:

> *"Wanted to let you know that the January info has been entered. The payroll numbers didn't account for the last 5 days of the month, so please add 16% and input them into your Google Form."*

Notice anything?
No link to the Google Form.

I was essentially told to get in my car and drive somewhere—without being given directions.
Oh, and for some reason, Google Forms is the navigation tool instead of, I don't know, *Sheets*, which is designed for tracking numbers.

So, I did the logical thing:

Me: *"Can you please send the Google Form to fill out?"*

Simple request, right?

Wrong.

## *STEP 2: THE ROADBLOCK (A.K.A., MY BOSS ALSO DIDN'T HAVE THE LINK)*

Instead of just sending me the link, my boss responded with this:

> *"The Google Form is in the manager month-end close email that goes out on the 1st. It is also in the reminder email I send out on the 7th. I'd recommend you bookmark it for easy access."*

Let's break this down.

I was asked to complete a task.
I asked for the missing link to complete said task.
Instead of just sending me the link, my boss told me to dig through old emails or wait several days for the reminder email to be sent.

Both options were:

- Absurd.

- Inefficient.

- A complete waste of company time and money.

At this point, it became clear:
My boss did not have the Google Form link either and just didn't want to admit it.

## *STEP 3: THE ROAD MAP SOLUTION*

Now, I had two options:

1. **Waste gas and drive in circles.** (*Dig through my inbox, search for a needle in a haystack, and lose precious time on a task that should take 5 seconds.*)
2. **Pull into a metaphorical rest stop and wait for clearer directions.** (*Do absolutely nothing and wait for the reminder email to drop the link directly into my inbox.*)

I chose option 2.

And guess what? A few days later, the email arrived with the link that should have just been sent to me in the first place.

**Lesson Learned: Sometimes, the best navigation choice is to park and wait.**

Not every roadblock is your problem to solve.

If leadership is running around in circles with no clear direction, let them exhaust themselves first.

Sometimes, the best way to "fix" inefficiency is to step aside and let them trip over their own incompetence.

## ROADBLOCK #2: The CFO & DOO Plan a Road Trip—But Forget the Map

Before we begin, let's go over who is supposed to be responsible for what:

**CFO** = Chief **FINANCIAL** Officer (responsible for **money**)
**DOO** = Director of **OPERATIONS** (responsible for **logistics**)
**Me** = Not either of those things

Got it? Cool. Now let's hit the road.

### *SETTING THE SCENE: THE ROAD TRIP IDEA*

> CFO: "Hey, Nikki, I wanted to get the conversation started on whether we could bring Cam on in a full-time position. I know Cam is at 24 hours in one department, and that's the max we can offer there. I'd like to have him work on marketing efforts (2-5 hrs per week). Are there other tasks we could throw at Cam to get him over 30 hours consistently?"
>
> Me: "Yes! We would definitely be able to keep him consistently above 30 hrs."

So far, so good. My bosses have an idea: Let's take Cam on a road trip to Full-Time Employment.

## *THE DETOUR: MISSING DIRECTIONS*

> CFO & DOO: "Cool. Can you summarize what his hours would look like across his duties? Do you have a proposed title? Would you propose a wage increase along with this offer? If so, please provide the expected payroll delta."

*Cue the brakes screeching.*

Who is responsible for financial planning? **CFO.**

Who is responsible for operational logistics? **DOO.**

Who was just asked to figure out the budget, the job title, the role structure, AND the payroll impact? **Me.** (A person who does not have the payroll budget, does not oversee marketing, and does not have the authority to set pay ranges.)

That's when it hit me: the map wasn't fully drawn. The idea was there, but the path forward? Not so much.

This is one of those moments where good intentions meet unclear execution. And it's more common than you'd think. Roles get blurry, responsibilities overlap, and suddenly, you're asked to fill in all the blanks—including ones that technically belong to someone else.

## *THE NAVIGATION DECISION: BUILD MY OWN MAP*

At that point, I had two choices:

**Option 1:** Scramble to guess what leadership *might* want and hope I check all the right boxes.

**Option 2:** Flip the script, center the employee, and build a plan based on what *Cam* actually wanted.

I chose option 2.

I sat down with Cam, talked through his goals, and created a structured, realistic job proposal—complete with hours breakdown, title, wage considerations, and (yes) the payroll math.

If I was being asked to drive, I was at least going to make sure we were headed somewhere that worked for my team—not just somewhere convenient for leadership.

**Lesson Learned:** If you're going to be handed the wheel, choose a destination that matters.

Sometimes, leaders have great ideas but haven't worked out the details yet. That's not failure—it's an opportunity to guide the conversation and advocate for your people.

If you're being asked to take the lead, use that moment to build something better—for your team, not just your higher-ups.

## FAKE ROADBLOCK #3: The $2 Bill Crisis of Leadership Incompetence

*(Or: When a Bro Boss Has a Complete Mental Breakdown Over Counting to Two)*

There are real roadblocks in management—budget constraints, staffing issues, and industry regulations.

And then there are fake roadblocks—rules and restrictions that exist for absolutely no reason other than someone once decided *that's just how it is.*

This is a story about the dumbest roadblock I have ever encountered.

**Meet Bro Boss.**

Bro Boss was exactly what you'd imagine.

- Jacked.

- Wore shirts two sizes too small.

- Did not drink protein shakes—he drank 'Brotiene Shakes.'

- Used phrases like "Get yoked" in professional settings.

His job?

Managing our daily financial closeouts. Counting cash. Entering numbers into a computer. A task that should be impossible to screw up.

And yet...

We were *never*, under *any* circumstances, allowed to accept a $2 bill.

Why?
He didn't know.
I didn't know.
No one knew.

I have worked many jobs in my lifetime. I have handled cash in multiple industries. And never, *not once*, had I heard of a ban on $2 bills.

At this point, I had two choices:
1.) Blindly follow this nonsense rule.
2.) Test the roadblock.

And so, one fateful day, I accepted a $2 bill.

Did I tell Bro Boss?
Absolutely not.

Instead, I hid it in the stack of ones.

Closeout time comes. Bro Boss starts counting the money.

Suddenly—

Bro Boss freezes.
Bro Boss stares at the $2 bill in horror.
Bro Boss stands up and yells:

"WHO DID THIS?"

He holds up the offending bill like it's a crime scene weapon.

"WHO PUT A TWO DOLLAR BILL IN THE STACK OF ONES?"

Silence. My coworkers and I sit in stunned disbelief because surely this is not happening.

But then—his entire demeanor shifts.
The rage drains from his body.
His arms go limp.
His face falls into pure panic.

And in the softest, most defeated voice I have ever heard, Bro Boss says:

"...I don't know how to proceed."

Let's pause for a moment.

This was our boss.
A fully grown adult.
A person in charge of money.

And he was not sure how to proceed because of a $2 bill.

At this point, the rest of us are still silent—mostly because we cannot believe what we are witnessing.

So what does Bro Boss do?
He calls HIS boss.

I kid you not.
This man picked up the phone to escalate this to corporate leadership.

And after actual discussion, after consultation with upper management, after exhausting all options—

Bro Boss finally learns that a $2 bill is counted as...
Two singles.

I, the chaos goblin that I am, immediately turned to my coworker and proudly declared:

"'Twas *I* who put the $2 bill in the stack of ones!"

### *The Aftermath*

I took that cursed $2 bill, exchanged it for two singles (*gasp!*), and laminated it with a note that says:

"Don't know how to proceed."

It now sits on my desk as a visual aid for my employees. Anytime someone comes to me with a problem I know they can solve on their own, I hand them the laminated $2 bill and tell them this story.

Lesson?

Test the roadblock.

If a rule makes no sense and no one can tell you why it exists, it is not a roadblock.
It is a speed bump masquerading as a pothole.
Drive right the fuck over it.

## The Poop-Colored Silver Lining of Navigating Managerial Nonsense

**1.) Sometimes, Leadership is Just a Fancy Word for "Making You Do Their Work."**
If your boss gives you vague instructions and expects you to fill in the blanks, congratulations—you've been promoted to Unofficial CEO of Managing Up.
**Solution:** Take control. If they're going to make you do the work, at least do it in a way that benefits you and your team.

**2.) If Your Boss Won't Hand You the Map, Make Your Own.**
When leadership can't give you basic tools (like a Google Form link) or expects you to navigate a mess they created,

you can either:

Waste time waiting for them to figure it out OR

Pave your own damn road and get where you need to go faster.

**Solution:** Work smarter, not harder. If leadership is lost, stop asking for directions and start making your own route.

### 3.) Most Roadblocks Are Fake. Just Drive Through.

If a rule, policy, or restriction makes no sense, and no one can explain why it exists, it's not real.

It's a fear-based, nonsense roadblock set up by someone who didn't know how to proceed.

**Solution:** Question everything. If the only reason a rule exists is "because it always has," then it's time to bulldoze right through it.

### 4.) The $2 Bill Rule Applies to Everything.

If a fully grown man in charge of finances can have a meltdown over counting to two, imagine how many other people in leadership are bullshitting their way through their jobs.

**Solution:** The next time your boss fumbles, remember: you are probably more competent than they are. Act accordingly.

### Final Takeaway:

Your bosses will stall, delegate, and panic their way through decisions. You don't have to.

**Be the driver, not the confused passenger.**

# | 8 |

# The Toxic Workplace Survival Guide

BECAUSE SOMETIMES, QUITTING
ISN'T AN OPTION...YET.

Welcome, weary corporate soldier.
You've found yourself in the trenches of workplace toxicity.

Whether it's incompetent leadership, backstabbing colleagues, or a company culture built on gaslighting and burnout, you are not alone.

But more importantly, you are not crazy.

Corporate bullshitery comes in many forms.

Sometimes, it's blatant.

Other times, it's so subtle and insidious that you don't even realize how bad things are until you wake up in a cold sweat, drafting emails in your sleep.

So, if you've ever thought:

**"Am I the problem?"** *(No, it's them.)*
**"Is my boss actually insane?"** *(Yes.)*
**"Why does this job feel like an emotionally abusive relationship?"** *(Because it probably is.)*

Then congratulations!
You officially work in a toxic environment.

But don't panic just yet.
This Survival Guide will help you keep your sanity intact while you plot your escape.
Or, at the very least, help you avoid committing a fireable offense before you find a new job.

## PHASE ONE: ORIENT YOURSELF IN THE HELLSCAPE

*(Understanding the Type of Toxicity You're Dealing With.)*

Before you start strategizing survival, you need to identify the specific brand of bullshit your workplace thrives on.

## Toxic Workplace Archetypes

**1.) The Gaslight Kingdom** *(Where the Problem Is Always YOU.)*
Your concerns are dismissed as "not a big deal."
You're constantly told, "You're overreacting."
The rules change daily, but you're expected to keep up.
If you push back, you're the difficult one.
Leadership's favorite phrase? "We're like a family." (RED FLAG)

**2.) The Burnout Cult** *(Where Hustle Culture Goes to Die.)*
"Work hard, play hard" is just code for 'we will grind you into the dirt.'
PTO? Technically, you have it, but good luck using it.
Employees brag about pulling all-nighters like it's a badge of honor.
There's always one guy who answers emails at 2 AM, and leadership calls him "a rockstar."

**3.) The Incompetence Circus** *(Where the Clowns Are in Charge.)*
Your boss has no idea how to do your job.
Leadership makes decisions based on vibes, not logic.
Every process is held together with duct tape, crossed fingers, and one employee who secretly does all the work.
You wonder daily how the company is still running.

**4.) The CYA (Cover Your Ass) Wasteland** *(Where Everything is Someone Else's Fault.)*
No one takes responsibility.

Every mistake is a game of Hot Potato—who can blame someone else first?

Important emails go *mysteriously missing.*

Someone is always throwing a colleague under the bus, and HR does nothing.

Once you identify the terrain, you can strategize accordingly.

(Or at least mentally prepare for the incoming bullshit.)

## PHASE TWO: SURVIVAL TACTICS (BEFORE YOU LOSE YOUR SOUL)

Now that you know what fresh corporate hell you're in, it's time to build your survival kit.

**Rule #1: Protect Your Sanity at All Costs.**

- **Detach emotionally.** Treat this job like an NPC side quest. Minimal emotional investment, maximum self-preservation.

- **Keep receipts.** If it's not in writing, it never happened. BCC yourself. Screenshot everything. Cover your ass.

- **Set boundaries like a motherfucker.** Your time off is sacred. Close your laptop. Silence Slack. Let them implode without you.

- **Embrace the clownery.** Some fights are not worth having. If management insists on a bad decision? Smile, nod, and let the fire burn.

## Rule #2: Stay One Step Ahead of the Bullshit.

- **Anticipate leadership's incompetence.** Make a Plan B before they inevitably ruin Plan A.

- **Get good at "managing up."** Dumb bosses need gentle nudges toward the right answer while believing it was their idea.

- **Strategically disappear.** If you're indispensable, they'll overload you. Become just useful enough but not the go-to fixer of everything.

## Rule #3: Master the Art of 'Corporate Combat.'

- **Match their energy.** If leadership thrives on meaningless buzzwords? Weaponize corporate jargon. (See: "We should circle back on that" = "I will never speak of this again.")

- **Master 'The Corporate No.'** Examples:

- "Can you take on this extra project?" → "Oh, I'd love to, but I don't have the bandwidth right now!"

- "Can you stay late?" → "I'm fully booked after hours, but I can revisit this tomorrow!"

- "Can you fix this thing that's not your job?" → "I'd be happy to support where I can—who should I loop in that actually owns this?"

## PHASE THREE: ESCAPE PLAN (BECAUSE THIS ISN'T SUSTAINABLE)

Look, you can only survive in a toxic workplace for so long. At some point, you need an exit strategy.

### _Signs It's Time to GTFO_

You dread work before you even wake up.
Your mental health is actively deteriorating.
You have no opportunities for growth.
You're not being paid enough for the bullshit.
You fantasize about flipping your desk and walking out mid-meeting.

### *The Escape Route*

Start job searching quietly. Update your résumé. Start networking. Get out before you're running on fumes.

Don't burn bridges (unless absolutely necessary). Leave on your terms, with a solid reference and a triumphant exit.

If HR is useless, get legal advice. If your workplace is hostile, discriminatory, or violating laws, lawyer up.

## Final Reality Check: Are You *Actually* in a Toxic Workplace?

*(Because Gaslighting is Real, and Sometimes You Need a Gut Check.)*

One of the hardest parts of working in a toxic environment? Sometimes, you don't even realize it's toxic.

Why? Because gaslighting works.

Because *"this is just how it is"* becomes a repeated mantra.

Because you get so deep in the bullshit that you forget what a normal job is supposed to feel like.

That's why whenever I check in with my staff, I don't ask, *"How are you feeling about work?"*

I don't ask, *"What are your frustrations?"*

Because people struggle to articulate workplace toxicity.

Instead, I ask:

"What's your workplace 80/20 at right now?"

### *The 80/20 Philosophy*

Nothing will ever be 100% good—that's not realistic.
But the ideal ratio we're aiming for? 80% good shit, 20% frustrating shit.
That's a manageable ratio. The good outweighs the bad.
Here's how you use this metric to check your workplace health:

**80% good, 20% bad** → This is *as good as it gets.* Normal frustrations exist, but overall, you feel valued, respected, and satisfied.

**70% good, 30% bad** → Still a solid workplace. There are some annoyances, but it's workable. Frustrations can likely be addressed and improved.

**60% good, 40% bad** → *Now we have a problem.* You're not miserable, but you're not happy either. At this stage, I tell my staff: *If you're feeling this dissatisfied, it might be time to start looking elsewhere.*

**50% good, 50% bad** → *Hard pause. Major evaluation time.* You should not feel this neutral about your job. Something fundamental is broken.

**Less than 50% good?** RUN. You are officially in a toxic workplace. You should not be here. Start your exit strategy now.

If you're sitting at 50/50 or worse and wondering:
*"Am I overreacting?"*

*"Am I making a big deal out of nothing?"*
*"But what if it's just me?"*

Stop.

You are not overreacting.
You deserve a job where the good outweighs the bad.
And if it doesn't?

That is your sign to leave.

## TL;DR: How to Know When to Get Out

**80/20** → *The dream. Stay here forever.*
**70/30** → *Still good. Problems? Yes. But manageable.*
**60/40** → *Getting dicey. Time to reflect.*
**50/50** → *Major red flag. Hard pause. Reevaluate everything.*
**Anything less than 50/50?** → *You're in a toxic workplace. It's time to leave.*

The reality is:
You can't always control the workplace, but you CAN control whether or not you stay in it.

# The Poop-Colored Silver Lining of Surviving a Toxic Workplace

Toxic jobs teach you something that healthy jobs often don't:

**What your boundaries actually are.**

You learn what you'll tolerate (and what you won't). You learn how to advocate for yourself—even when leadership won't. You learn how to spot red flags faster than ever before. You learn that staying silent to keep the peace never works in the long run. And most importantly?

You learn that *quitting* isn't failure—it's self-preservation.

No one gets out of a toxic workplace without a few emotional bruises. But if you're lucky, you walk away with sharper instincts, higher standards, and the absolute refusal to settle for anything less than a workplace that respects the hell out of you.

That's not weakness. That's a power-up.

# | 9 |

# Neurodiversity in the Workplace

## DEI: JUST ANOTHER BOX TO CHECK

Alright, let's start with a disclaimer:
I'm not a workplace lawyer. I don't claim to have a comprehensive understanding of what discrimination looks like to everyone.

This chapter is about the times I've personally experienced workplace discrimination—not in the form of outright hostility, but in the death-by-a-thousand-cuts style that many neurodivergent employees deal with daily.

And look, I get it—workplace discrimination is a broad and deeply complex issue. Many marginalized groups experience it in far more overt and damaging ways than I have.

But the point of this chapter isn't just to vent.

It's to showcase the gap between companies that claim to support diversity, equity, and inclusion and the reality of how they actually function.

Because companies love to shout about DEI.

- They make employees complete mandatory training.
- They post about their progressive hiring initiatives on LinkedIn.
- They declare themselves a "safe and inclusive workplace."

But the moment real inclusivity requires them to change how they operate—to actually adjust for diverse ways of thinking, working, and communicating?

Suddenly, that diversity becomes an inconvenience.

Here's what companies don't tell you: supporting DEI means more than checking a hiring box. It means making room for *how* people work—not just *who* they are.

And when they refuse to do that? You end up stuck in the kind of maddening double standard that neurodivergent professionals know all too well...

# Tone Policing: The Neurodivergent Catch-22

I communicate directly and prefer to be communicated with in clear, straightforward ways.

Yet, at one company I worked for, my direct communication style was frequently criticized.
I was told I'm "blunt and intimidating."

Here's the Catch-22 of Being Neurodivergent in the Workplace:

- If you communicate directly, you're "too harsh."
- If you soften your tone, you risk sounding uncertain or less authoritative.
- If you try to strike a balance, neurotypicals still interpret your words based on their own biases rather than your intent.

And if you're both neurodivergent and a woman? Forget it.

- If a male leader speaks bluntly, he's seen as "assertive" and "efficient."
- If a woman does the same, she's "aggressive" and "intimidating."

## *Case in Point: The Roger Situation*

One of my bosses once requested a Friday meeting with me and one of my employees, Roger.

I responded with a neutral, factual statement:
 *"Roger doesn't work on Fridays."*

That's it. No sass. No exasperation. Just a fact.

My boss's response? A full-blown wrist-slap wrapped up in an email:

> *"Hey Nikki, I have some feedback concerning the tone of your email, as it comes off as impatient and exasperated to me.*
>
> *I do not have the schedules of your staff memorized, and I do not know when Roger works or doesn't work as he does not report to me. Your email came off as you being annoyed that I was requesting a meeting.*
>
> *Going forward, the way I would prefer to be communicated to would be giving me the options/context in your original response. So instead of 'Roger doesn't work on Fridays,' it would have been more useful to say:*
>
> *'Roger doesn't work on Fridays, but here are other options when I know he and I will be able to meet...*"

### *The Takeaway?*

I stated a neutral fact. My boss perceived it as an emotional outburst.

In corporate America, directness = rudeness—but only if you're neurodivergent (or a woman).

***Mini Lesson:*** *If a neutral statement from a neurodivergent employee reads as "rude," the issue isn't tone—it's bias.*

---

# The "Fix Yourself to Make Us Comfortable" Feedback Loop

---

The same company hosted yearly leadership retreats.
(If you missed my thoughts on those, I recommend *circling back* to Chapter 4: The Corporate Circus of Bullshit.)

For three years straight, after every single retreat, I was pulled aside and told:
"Can I offer you some feedback?"

And that feedback always boiled down to:

- *Getting scolded for "not looking engaged."* → (I engage by fidgeting.)

- *Criticized for "asking pointed questions."* → (I need clear, concrete answers to understand things.)

- *Asked why I "don't make direct eye contact."* → (It makes me really uncomfortable to do that.)

- *Told I should "want to be in close proximity to coworkers."* → (...what??)

After three years of getting the same "fix yourself" list, I had to wonder—

Did they want a leader or a corporate Stepford Wife?

Every comment chipped away at my sense of security—until eventually, I stopped showing up as myself.

I TRIED to change.
I really did.
And it tanked my mental health.

Because here's the truth:

- I was one of the highest performers in the company.
- My team ran more efficiently than any other.
- My department had better engagement, fewer problems, and higher retention.

Yet, because my mannerisms and communication style made neurotypicals uncomfortable, I was expected to change.

That's not inclusion.

**Mini Lesson:** *Performance is measurable. Personality is not. Don't let vague "feedback" invalidate concrete results.*

## When "Inclusion" Requires Disclosure

At this point, I had two options:

1.) Get frustrated and keep quiet.
2.) Take the high road and use this as a teaching moment.

I figured if leadership was truly invested in inclusivity, I could challenge them to think about how they engage with neurodivergent employees.

So, instead of brushing it off, I sent an email breaking down why direct communication isn't a problem and how asking employees to "soften their tone" can be a form of masking—something widely recognized as detrimental to neurodivergent individuals (Raymaker et al., 2020).

I even provided research-backed resources on how neurodivergent employees thrive in environments that prioritize:

- Clear expectations

- Direct feedback

- Structured communication

I expected reflection. Maybe even a meaningful conversation about workplace culture. What I got instead?

> "I agree that masking isn't helpful...but have you considered sharing your neurodivergence with the team?"

Not only was I encouraged to disclose private medical information, but I was also asked how I'd prefer to do it—
A group meeting?
1:1 conversations?
Some other venue?

Hard stop.

If any employer ever encourages, asks, or even *suggests* that you disclose personal health information?

THAT IS NOT LEGAL.

This wasn't "inclusion."
This wasn't "understanding."
This was a corporate leadership team trying to offload the discomfort of their own biases onto me.

And that? That is exactly why DEI efforts fall apart the moment they require actual change.

## The Poop-Colored Silver Lining: Being the Change (Even When Your Bosses Suck at It)

The reality of corporate DEI is harsh but simple:
*Companies love to hire for diversity but refuse to adapt for it.*
They pat themselves on the back for "inclusivity" while still forcing employees to conform to outdated norms.
They want different perspectives—just as long as those perspectives sound exactly like theirs.

But here's the thing:
You don't have to play by their rules.

If leadership refuses to build an environment where diverse minds can thrive, be the leader who does.

Make space for different communication styles.
Challenge corporate bullshit when you see it.
Be the manager you wish you had.

Because the next generation of employees deserve better than DEI as a buzzword.

And if your company refuses to get with the times?

There's always another workplace that will.

# | 10 |

# Times I've Fucked Up

## (AND WHAT I'VE LEARNED FROM FUCKING UP)

Yep, I've fucked up a lot. If you've made it this far in the book, you should have picked up on the fact that I'm basically an agent of chaos. I have a morbid curiosity with stirring the pot, and often, the filter between my brain and my mouth doesn't function properly. All that being said, it simply wouldn't be fair to write a book completely shitting on management, corporate bullshit, and incompetent bosses without also highlighting the times I, too, made stupid decisions.

## Bonus Structure is Bullshit

One time, in a full-company meeting—with the CEO, CFO, DOO, and every department head present—I casually announced that the way bonuses were allocated was stupid. Just threw it right out there. Unfiltered. No warning. No regrets…until later.

The structure was simple: if the company as a whole profited, everyone got a bonus. If it didn't, no one did. In theory, fine. In practice? My location consistently crushed it while other facilities, from my very biased perspective, sat around twiddling their thumbs. So, I said what I said. I may have also implied that my team worked harder than everyone else (because we did). I thought I was stating facts. Leadership thought I was issuing a declaration of war.

The best part of this story? The backlash. I just wanted acknowledgment that my team was killing it. Instead, I got a stern talking-to from one of my bosses and was told I needed to "apologize to my coworkers" for insinuating that I work harder than them. (I wasn't "insinuating" anything—I made that point loud and clear.) My boss followed up with me every Friday thereafter until I apologized to all my coworkers for my behavior.

Lesson learned: Pick your battles. Pick your audience. And maybe—just maybe—don't start a war in a full-company meeting.

And while that moment was a very public facepalm, some of my biggest regrets didn't happen under a spotlight. They happened behind closed doors—when I had to make hard calls as a manager.

## Regret Over Firing Two Employees

At this point in my career, I've fired a lot of employees. Very seldom do I question my decision to let someone go—usually because there are clear policies that were violated or issues that were obviously fireable offenses. But there are two terminations that still, to this day, do not sit right with me.

Let me be clear—letting these employees go was **100% the correct decision** in both scenarios. However, looking back, I wish I had handled both instances with more grace and kindness.

### *Employee 1: The Overachiever Who Couldn't Make It to Work on Time*

Jace was, honestly, a fantastic employee. He had great vibes, handled difficult situations well, was a favorite among our clients, and my staff looked to him as an unofficial leader in their department. He had all the makings to go somewhere in the industry—if he wanted to. Unfortunately, from my perspective, it didn't seem like he wanted to go anywhere because he had a painful track record of constantly showing up late for work.

While this drove me crazy (because timeliness is *important*, people), none of my staff cared. They loved Jace. He made the workplace enjoyable. And yet, I stuck to my guns and terminated him for recurring tardiness.

What I didn't anticipate was the backlash. Staff were confused and upset with me. Clients were frustrated. And suddenly, it felt like I had fired a local celebrity.

The mistake I made? Not being transparent. I should have followed up with staff about what led me to terminate Jace and why his patterns of tardiness were a bigger issue than what they saw. Instead, I gave them a generic "he broke policy" response, which didn't do much to help them understand. I really wish I had been more clear about why this decision was necessary rather than spewing policy jargon at them.

### *Employee 2: The Underachiever Who Never Did Anything Wrong...But Also Never Did Anything Right*

While I regret how I handled Jace's termination because I failed to communicate the full picture, I regret Jimmy's firing for the opposite reason—I knew exactly why I wanted him gone, but I wasn't honest about it.

Jimmy followed every policy to a T. He was always on time. He did his job. But the problem? He had a shit attitude and a huge ego. Like, toxic levels bad.

- He whispered in staff's ears about my incompetence as a boss.
- He told everyone he could do a better job than management.
- He questioned every decision I made but never brought those concerns up to me.
- He shit-talked the company loudly in front of clients.

Obviously, not cool. And his sour attitude tanked morale for the rest of my staff.

Jimmy needed to go. BUT I had no real "fireable" offense. I tried talking to him, informing him that the negativity needed to stop. But in every conversation, he swore he LOVED working for me and LOVED his job (*pro tip—don't bullshit your boss; we know the truth*).

So, I scrapped together a pretty pathetic reason to fire him: he wasn't meeting the required number of shifts per week to stay on payroll. While this was technically true, I know that if it had been any other employee, I would have found a way to work with them.

Jimmy was, rightfully, pissed. He took to social media to air his grievances. That act alone cemented that I made the right decision. HOWEVER, I wish I had documented his poor attitude more thoroughly so I could have provided the real reason for termination instead of scrambling for a weak excuse.

Lesson learned: Document everything. And if someone needs to go, be honest about why.

## The Time My Own Policies (Or Lack Thereof) Bit Me in the Ass

When my brand-new, multi-million-dollar, state-of-the-art rock climbing facility opened, I knew one thing for sure: I wanted my dogs in the office. So, I structured my policies to reflect that service dogs were welcome, but I purposefully failed to mention anything about non-service animals. My *clever* little loophole.

What I failed to realize was that my staff noticed every time I brought my dogs to work. At some point, they also noticed that our policies didn't explicitly state that *only* service dogs were allowed.

So, naturally, other people started bringing their dogs to work.

Which, in concept? Sounds great. In practice? A lawsuit waiting to happen.

Things spiraled when random gym members started trying to bring their dogs, too. At that point, I had to eat crow and update the policy to clearly state that only service animals were welcome.

Lesson learned: As a leader, you absolutely need to follow all of your own rules. If you bend them for yourself, people will notice. And if you're going to bend the rules, at least be smart enough to write yourself a loophole in the first place.

Okay, so I *may or may not* have grandfathered my dogs into the new policy. But hey—some exceptions are worth the risk.

## The Poop-Colored Silver Lining of all my Fuck Ups

**1.) The Bonus Meltdown** → I Learned That Timing & Delivery Matter.

Sometimes you *can* be right, but if you say it in the wrong way, *you still lose.*

You don't get validation by *demanding* it. You get it by playing the long game. (Annoying, but true.)

You can either be *effective* or *sassy in a company-wide meeting.* Unfortunately, not both.

**2.) Firing Jace & Jimmy** → I Learned That Transparency & Documentation Matter.

Employees aren't just numbers—they're part of a bigger team dynamic that people *actually* care about.

It's not enough to follow policy—you also need to communicate decisions clearly so people understand *why.*

If someone is being a toxic gremlin, document everything. Because when the time comes, you don't want to be grasping at weak excuses (*cough* Jimmy *cough*).

**3.) The Dog Policy Disaster** → I Learned That Leaders Set the Tone.

If you break your own rules, people will notice—and they will follow.

Even the *smallest* personal exception can snowball into absolute chaos.

If you're gonna bend the rules for yourself, at least write in a clever loophole upfront.

# | 11 |

# When The Office isn't just a Sitcom

## BUT RATHER, IT'S YOUR ACTUAL LIFE

Have you ever wondered what it would be like to have Michael Scott as a boss? Do you think it would be fun working in an environment of constant pranks and shenanigans? I'd wager a bet that at least one person reading this has worked under a Michael Scott at some point. And the truth of the matter is—it *is* fun! ...at first.

But at some point, the jokes go too far. At some point, your employees want to develop, get pay raises, and achieve something productive...not partake in office-wide Nerf wars.

Anyway, this chapter is dedicated entirely to a Michael Scott boss I had at one point in my career. And yes, *every single one of these stories is real.* Because it just seems fitting, I'm going to go ahead and refer to this boss as Michael.

## The Nerf Wars

Michael had an arsenal of Nerf guns in his office. Not even kidding—this was a weapons range of foam-based warfare. He had different types of Nerf ammo, an array of Nerf guns, and even a Nerf bow and arrow (honestly, that one was hands down the coolest). He prided himself on his collection, with some of his *"big guns"* mounted on the wall like trophies.

*(As I'm writing this, I really wish I were making all this up. I probably don't need to foreshadow anything, but believe it or not, this story gets worse, or better, depending on the type of chaos goblin you are.)*

It was Michael's life mission—and possibly his sole source of joy—to shoot us at the worst and most inappropriate times.

- Talking to a client? *Michael sniped you.* Headshots were worth extra points. Bonus points if the client didn't notice. (*Spoiler: They always noticed.*)
- Waiting for a document to print? *Michael would NINJA RUN and dive under desks* so you wouldn't see

him coming before he ambushed you with his Nerf machine gun.

- Eating your lunch in the break room? *Michael would lift the ceiling tiles connecting the offices to the break room*—and shoot you from above.

As you can imagine, not everyone took kindly to being shot at while trying to accomplish their daily responsibilities.

So, staff started bringing in their own Nerf guns to work. What followed was a full-blown rebellion—an organized movement against Michael's reign of terror.

What began as workplace sniper shots escalated into a war zone.

- You had to check behind doors before entering a room because there was a HIGH likelihood that someone was waiting to ambush you.
- Michael built a barricade out of boxes.
- Staff, fully committed, charged the barricade like they were storming the Bastille.
- Someone literally sang 'One Day More' from *Les Misérables* before a full-scale office siege commenced.

## *The Day I Broke*

While all this *corporate warfare* was unfolding in the offices, I was in the middle of getting my lift certification.

*(Yes, remember that misogynistic electrician? This training was the exact reason why I knew more than he did.)*

For my certification, I had to demonstrate that I could pull a boom lift into the building and raise the platform to certain heights. And because *actual safety matters,* I was being tested by a professional instructor to make sure I wasn't about to commit workplace manslaughter.

So, there I was, 50 feet up in a lift basket with a random industry professional administering my test.

And then, out of nowhere...

WHAM. I took a Nerf dart to the head.

WHAM. A split second later, *random industry professionals* also took a headshot.

I glanced over. Random Industry Professional glared at me. We both inched toward the edge of the lift basket, peered over—and there, rolling on the ground laughing so hard he was crying, was Michael.

I looked back at Random Industry Professional and sighed.

"I'm not passing this test, am I?"

"Nope."

For clarity's sake, I didn't technically fail because I got sniped mid-test. I failed because Michael, the actual child that he was, entered my work zone while I was operating heavy machinery, thus creating a safety hazard.

And because I didn't set up a safety perimeter, I was deemed "at fault" for the failure.

Which, frankly, was bullshit.

So, I did the only thing that made sense—I rounded up every last Nerf gun in the entire building, packed them into boxes, and hid them in the very back of a storage closet.

And THEN, I retook my lift test.

I passed with flying colors.

### *Moral of the Story?*

I honestly don't know. Maybe it's:

- If your boss shows up to work with a Nerf gun, it's a red flag.

- If your workplace resembles a LARP war zone, it's *probably* time to rethink things.

- If your lift certification gets derailed because your boss thinks mid-test sniper shots are hilarious, then yeah—you might be working in a real-life sitcom.

But all I know for sure? If I ever see an office stocked with Nerf guns again, I'm walking out the door.

## Hide the Dildo - Michael's Idea of Team Bonding

The title of this section is exactly what it sounds like—HR's nightmare.

Michael had an earth-shatteringly genius idea to engage staff and boost morale:

He would hide a dildo, and staff would...find it.

I'm really sorry for the details I'm about to provide. I wouldn't be doing my job as a storyteller if I didn't set the scene properly.

This wasn't a cute, discreet little dildo that could be easily pushed out of sight if a customer was around. No, this was an at-least-9-inch, porn-star-level girth, horrifyingly realistic dildo.

Please keep those details in mind as you continue reading.

Michael took pride in finding the most uncomfortable places for an employee to stumble across the dildo.

- Helping a client try on shoes? *Open box—no shoes, but dildo.*
- Going to grab a sticky note? *Open drawer—dildo.*
- Counting cash at the end of shift? *Open safe—dildo.*

You get the idea.

And then...the dildo disappeared. The game *seemingly* stopped. But that felt off-brand for Michael.

Oh, it was. He had found the ultimate hiding place. And he was just...waiting.

Fast forward to post-COVID, when we were making adjustments to the facility, one task involved removing an old turnstile to improve the flow of traffic at the entrance.

An employee was disassembling the turnstile when he noticed something large, pink, and rubber lodged inside the mechanical components.

He called us over. Expecting to see a dead mouse or something equally gross, we gathered around—only for him to slowly unsheath a giant dildo from the turnstile, holding it aloft like Excalibur.

"I WON! I WON HIDE THE DILDO!" he proclaimed.

Michael was crying with laughter.

This all happened in front of paying customers.

Just take a moment to realize that at some point, Michael had fully disassembled the turnstile to hide the dildo inside—then reassembled it without any of us noticing.

I don't know exactly how this story ends because I submitted my resignation letter shortly after.

Moral of the story? Companies have HR for a reason. If something like this is happening in your workplace, you should probably bring it to HR's attention.

**Mini Lesson:** *If a prank could be considered evidence in an HR case, it's probably not a "fun team activity."*

## The Hamster and The GoPro

I don't like this story.
Mainly because it's borderline animal cruelty (don't come for me, PETA—I had nothing to do with it).

One day, Michael decided it would be *hilarious* to play a prank on another manager.
So he:

- Cleared out the manager's desk drawer

- Filled it with small animal bedding, food, water, and a hamster wheel

- Put a real, live hamster inside

- AND placed a GoPro in the drawer to film the reaction

That's right.
Michael gift-wrapped an actual live rodent as a surprise and thought, "Yeah. This is workplace humor."

Well, the manager opened the drawer, stared at the hamster, sighed deeply, and closed it again.
Because, at that point, he was over it.

Michael thought this was *hysterical.*

The manager?
Burnt out. Tired. Overworked. Undervalued.
A surprise hamster wasn't going to fix that.
What he *actually* wanted was a raise, career development, and to feel like his work mattered.
He didn't want a desk pet.

And here's the hard truth about working for a boss like Michael:
At some point, the "fun workplace" stops being fun.
People want growth. They want opportunities. They want to be taken seriously.
And when leadership prioritizes pranks over professional

development?
That's when employees check out.

Oh! And because I know you're wondering—
The hamster was fine and ended up going home with an employee's kid.
So, I guess this story has a happy ending...for the hamster, at least.

## The Poop-Colored Silver Lining of Working in an Actual Sitcom

1.) Creating a *fun* workplace is important—but fun should *complement* professionalism, not replace it.

2.) Your employees will, at some point, want to grow. That's not a problem—it's a *gift*. Nurture it. Reward it. Don't try to distract from it with foam darts and desk hamsters.

3.) Dildos don't belong in the workplace. Period. Unless you work at a sex shop. In which case—respectfully—carry on.

**The real joke?** A boss like Michael thinks he's the life of the party. But in reality, he's the reason people leave early.

# SO, YOU STILL WANT TO BE A MANAGER?

If you've made it to the end of this book, I can only assume one of three things:

1. You're already a manager, and this book either made you feel deeply seen or gave you PTSD flashbacks.
2. You're about to become a manager, and you're now questioning every life choice that led you here.
3. You just really enjoy reading about absolute workplace absurdity.

Either way, welcome to the club.

## So, What's the Takeaway?

Managing people is not for the faint of heart.
It's not glamorous. It's not just about leadership.
It's not about "changing the world" like LinkedIn influencers want you to believe.

It's about navigating absolute chaos while trying to keep the ship from sinking.
It's about picking your battles, choosing your words wisely, and somehow keeping your sanity intact.
It's about laughing through the absurdity—because if you don't, you'll cry.

### The Real Secret to Management?

It's not about buzzwords.
It's not about goal-setting.
It's not even about surviving corporate clownery.

It's about the people you lead.

The absolute only thing that makes this job worth it is building a team that trusts you, respects you, and knows you've got their back.

Your job is not to fix the system (because, let's be honest, the system is fundamentally broken).
*Your job is to make the work environment suck less for the people in it.*

At the end of the day, that's the only part of leadership that truly matters.


### Final Thoughts: Was It Worth It?

Was all the bullshit, clownery, buzzword bingo, and headache-inducing absurdity worth it?

For me? 100% yes.

Because through all of it—the broken systems, the dumpster fires, the managerial nightmares—I got to build some truly incredible teams.

Someone had to deal with all the nonsense, the corporate circus, and the HR nightmares.

And honestly? I'm glad it was me.

I'm glad I got to be the one to cut through the bullshit, advocate for my staff, and create policies that actually held people accountable.

I'm glad I got to lead with an employee-first mindset and give my team the opportunities they deserved.

So, if you're like me—if you have a keen eye for bullshit and zero patience for corporate fluff, then management is going to be tough.

But if you're also like me—a snarky chaos goblin who will always put their team first, then you're going to thrive.

Because at the end of the day?

The system is broken. But your leadership doesn't have to be.


### *Now go forth. Lead well.*

And for the love of god, don't let your boss start a workplace dildo scavenger hunt.

# About the Author

## Where to Find Me After This Shitstorm

So, after reading this absolute trainwreck of a book, you might be wondering:
Who the hell is this person, and why does she have so many stories about butts, dildos, and corporate nonsense?

Fair question.

**Hi. I'm Nikki.**
I've spent over a decade managing rock climbing gyms, fitness facilities, and teams of absolute gremlins (whom I love dearly).

Along the way, I realized that:

1. Most management books are boring as hell.
2. No one actually prepares you for what leadership is REALLY like.
3. There's a serious gap between "corporate best practices" and "how to survive absolute chaos."

So, I wrote this book.

But my work doesn't stop here.
After years of dealing with corporate dysfunction, I decided to build something better.

## ~Welcome to Altuum ~

A consultancy designed to help climbing gyms & fitness facilities actually function.

No corporate fluff. No nonsense. Just real, practical solutions for better systems, better leadership, and better businesses.

If you liked this book and want to see how I help gyms get their shit together—minus the literal shit (though I do seem to specialize in that too)—you can find me here:

https://www.altuumconsultancy.com/

**Otherwise?**

Enjoy your job (or quit it).

May the force be with you and may you never have to approve time off for a second butthole surgery.

**Learn More About Altuum**